JUST LED ZEPPELIN REAL BOOK Complete

MW00806053

Project Managers: CAROL CUELLAR and AARON STANG

Music Editors: BILL GALLIFORD, ETHAN NEUBURG, COLGAN BRYAN, and AARON STANG

Arrangers: ETHAN NEUBURG, JACKIE WORTH, and KEVIN MacKELVIE

Guitar Transcriptions: ANDY ALEDORT

Production Coordinator: SHERYL ROSE

Technical Editor: JACK ALLEN

Additional Editorial: ANDY ALEDORT

Engraver: MARK BURGESS

Photos courtesy of STAR FILE

Cover: MARTHA L. RAMIREZ and JORGE PAREDES

Due to copyright restrictions, we are unable to include "We're Gonna Groove" in this collection.

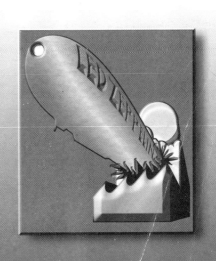

Contents

Introduction

By Andy Aledort

In the world of popular music, one band stands alone atop rock's Mt. Olympus as the unrivaled champion and absolute master of the form: Led Zeppelin. Jimmy Page (guitar, vocals, producer), Robert Plant (lead vocals), John Paul Jones (bass, vocals), and John Bonham (drums, vocals) joined forces in 1968 to form Led Zeppelin, and from its inception the group transformed rock 'n' roll into something new and different—threatening, exhilarating, mysterious, gut-wrenching—with eight ground-breaking LPs released over an 11-year span. In the process, Led Zeppelin set the precedent for a brand-new musical sound and style that would become known as heavy metal.

Guitarist Jimmy Page (b. 1944), the mastermind behind Led Zeppelin, was something of a child prodigy. As a young teen he appeared on English national television performing skiffle music (a hard-driving style of acoustic music rooted in American folk, New Orleans jazz and jug-band styles), and by 1963, Page had proven his mettle as England's number-one session guitarist, at times working three sessions a day, six days a week. Through the mid-'60s, Page appeared on hundreds of studio recordings with artists such as The Who, The Kinks, Tom Jones, Donovan, and Nico.

Bassist/multi-instrumentalist John Paul Jones (John Baldwin, b. 1946) was also a successful session musician, arranging and performing many British hit songs during the '60s for the Rolling Stones, Herman's Hermits, and Dusty Springfield. While working together on Donovan's 1968 *Hurdy Gurdy Man* sessions, Page and Jones decided to follow the lead of successful three-piece heavy rock bands like Cream and the Jimi Hendrix Experience to form their own three-piece unit plus a vocalist.

Since 1966, Page had been a member of the Yardbirds, initially performing on bass but moving to guitar for a brief period alongside Jeff Beck. Upon Beck's departure in '67, Page became the band's principal guitarist. While forming his new group with Jones, Jimmy's initial choice for vocals, Terry Reid, suggested instead wailing blues vocalist/harmonica player Robert Plant (b. 1948), who in turn brought along drummer John Bonham (1948–1980), his band-mate from the defunct Band of Joy. Page, Plant, Jones, and Bonham toured Scandinavia in the fall of '68 as the New Yardbirds, changing their name to Led Zeppelin following Who drummer Keith Moon's derisive remark that they went over like a "lead zeppelin."

At the end of '68, the group entered London's Olympic Studios and emerged 30 hours later with their smash debut, *Led Zeppelin* (Atlantic). *Led Zeppelin* is an eclectic offering including bone-rattling covers of Chicago blues classics such as Muddy Waters' "You Shook Me" and Otis Rush's "I Can't Quit You Baby," blues-drenched proto-metal originals such as the brilliant "Dazed and Confused" and "How Many More Times," the traditional folk song "Babe I'm Gonna Leave You," an original take on English folk–meets–Indian classical music with "Black Mountain Side" (originally titled "White Summer"), and metal-grinding power-pop like "Good Times, Bad Times" and the full-throttle "Communication Breakdown."

With the formation of Led Zeppelin, Page's artistic sensibilities exploded. As leader, principal songwriter, guitarist, arranger, engineer, and producer, Page found in Led Zeppelin a mighty vehicle with which to obliterate the competition. As Page explains, "The Yardbirds allowed me to improvise a lot and I started building a textbook of ideas that I eventually used in Led Zeppelin. I wanted Zeppelin to be a marriage of blues, hard rock, and acoustic music, topped with heavy choruses—a combination that had never been done before." By combining elements of blues, folk, R&B/soul, and Indian classical with a fearless, envelope-breaking artistic sensibility, Page and company forged sounds and musical styles never before heard. The band also devised tight, well-thought-out arrangements, using drastic extremes in dynamics. More than 20 years have passed since the dissolution of the original line-up, but the recordings of Led Zeppelin still stand as the most substantial, forward-looking, and influential rock music of all time.

A prime factor in the impact and ultimate success of Led Zeppelin was its finely honed, immediately recognizable sound. Each component—guitar, voice, bass, and drums—was presented with incredible vibrancy and depth. Bonham's superhuman drumming—described by Cream bassist Jack Bruce as "the best drum sound ever recorded"—on cuts like "Good Times, Bad Times" was further propelled by Jones' earth-shaking, virtuoso bass playing.

Over this rock-solid bed, Plant and Page respectively supplied peeling vocals and searing guitar work. Page also devised innovative studio techniques such as backward and hard-panned reverb effects. The band members had final say on every aspect of their career, including the innovative design work for the album covers; as Page has bluntly stated, "I wanted artistic control in a vise grip." Within two months of its release, *Led Zeppelin* was sweeping the global airwaves.

Ten months later emerged *Led Zeppelin II,* a certified masterwork that verified the ambitious scope of Led Zeppelin's musical vision. The album is weighted toward brilliantly devised hard rock, exemplified by the tracks "Whole Lotta Love," "Heartbreaker," "Living Loving Maid," "Moby Dick," and "Ramble On," with futuristic blues songs like "The Lemon Song" and "Bring It On Home" balanced against the more pop-like "What Is and What Should Never Be" and "Thank You."

Though the band never released singles, the churning "Whole Lotta Love" was played in heavy rotation on FM radio despite its more than five-and-a-half-minute length and the fact that the majority of the song is a musical collage of tape effects, Theremin (an early synthesizer-like device), and Robert Plant's testosterone-induced grunting and groaning.

Zeppelin's liberal borrowing of musical themes and lyrics, however—from Muddy Waters' "You Need Love" on "Whole Lotta Love" and Robert Johnson's "Traveling Riverside Blues" and Elmore James' "Killing Floor" on "The Lemon Song"—instigated a slew of lawsuits, most of which were settled out of court. But there was no denying the impact and worldwide adoration Led Zeppelin had now achieved. Constant touring for two years helped *Led Zeppelin II* hit number one on the charts; incredibly, the band would score number ones with each of its next five releases.

On *Led Zeppelin III,* the group expanded its sonic palette even further, delving deeper into the acoustic sounds of folk and country on the tracks "Tangerine," "Gallows Pole," and "Hats Off to (Roy) Harper," plus instilling Indian motives once again on "Friends." Though some fans derided the band's acoustic leanings, *Zep III* also contains the brutally intense "Immigrant Song," one of rock's heaviest tracks, as well at the darkly soulful and emotive "Since I've Been Loving You," the most original and effective incorporation of blues stylings in the band's catalog. Other powerful cuts are "Out on the Tiles" (reminiscent of the Yardbirds' "Shapes of Things") and "Bron-Y-Aur Stomp."

The band's fearless approach to using recording studio technology would also come in handy, one example being the bizarre synthesizer overlap from the outro of "Friends" into the intro of "Celebration Day." In this instance, necessity was the mother of invention when Bonham's drum tracks at the beginning of "Celebration Day" were accidentally erased, forcing Page to come up with a solution. The result is a jarring effect of Bonham's drums dropping in suddenly in the middle of the first verse.

With the release of *Led Zeppelin IV* in November '71, everything else the band had done up to that point represented the mere tip of the iceberg. *Led Zeppelin IV,* on the strength of the FM staple and certified masterpiece "Stairway to Heaven," is revered as one of the all-time greatest albums in rock, alongside Jimi Hendrix's *Electric Ladyland,* the Beatles' *Sgt. Pepper's Lonely Hearts Club Band,* and The Who's *Tommy.*

The album also marked the beginning of the band's so-called obsession with mysticism and the occult, a claim firmly denied by Jimmy Page. Part of this impression stems from the four mystical, rune-like symbols that adorn the inside of the album jacket. Each symbol was either chosen or designed by one of the band members, and the meaning of these symbols has been a subject of debate among Zep fanatics.

One of the many standout tracks from *Led Zeppelin IV* is "When the Levee Breaks," which features a crushing drum sound from Bonham. Page explains, "I had been exploring the use of ambient miking techniques for the drums, like placing [mikes] in hallways, far from the drums, which is how we got the sound on 'When the Levee Breaks.'"

Led Zeppelin IV also assured Page's stance as an undisputed rock guitar deity, as he displayed pyrotechnical guitar mastery on the blazing tracks "Rock and Roll," "Black Dog," and the archetypal "Stairway to Heaven."

Led Zeppelin followed the artistic and commercial success of *Zep IV* with the early '73 release of *Houses of the Holy,* an album ingeniously conceived, performed, recorded, and produced. The album's impressive opening cut, "The Song Remains the Same," started out as an instrumental titled "The Overture," which was to serve as an intro to Page's majestic "The Rain Song." Solid from top to bottom, the impressive songwriting and performing abilities of Zeppelin on *Houses* are elucidated by the tracks "Over the Hills and Far Away," "Dancing Days," "No Quarter," and "The Ocean."

Worldwide success and constant touring did little to slow the creative juggernaut of Led Zeppelin at its peak, and the group's next release, 1975's *Physical Graffiti,* was a double set of great consistency. Though this album is primarily made up of new material, a few of the tracks came from previous sessions: "The Rover" and "Black Country Woman" were from the *Houses of the Holy* sessions; "Down by the Seaside," "Boogie With Stu," and "Night Flight" were from the *Zep IV* sessions; and "Bron-Yr-Aur" was from the *Zep III* sessions.

Not as "produced"-sounding as *Houses, Physical Graffiti* is an album of substantial depth and range. As Page puts it, "I think this album is really honest. *Physical* is more personal, and I think it allows the listener to enter our world." *Physical Graffiti* contains some of the band's greatest performances—very raw and alive—as well as ambitious and compelling compositions such as "Kashmir," "In the Light," "Ten Years Gone," "Trampled Under Foot," "Houses of the Holy," and the haunting "In My Time of Dying."

August 4, 1975, Robert Plant suffered a near-fatal car accident. While still ailing, he and the band entered the studio and in just 18 days cut *Presence,* which went on to sell more than four million copies. The album's standouts include "Achilles Last Stand," "Nobody's Fault but Mine," and "Tea for One." Tragically, Plant's six-year-old son Karac died of a viral infection shortly thereafter, forcing the cancellation of the tour and a period of dormancy for the band.

In 1976, Zeppelin released the double-live *The Song Remains the Same,* the soundtrack to a concert film. *The Song Remains the Same* film combined footage of the band's 1973 tour and dream sequences written by each member of the band, and was another well-charting success.

Nearly four years passed before the band issued its final studio effort, 1979's *In Through the Out Door,* which included the FM favorite "All My Love." September 25, 1980, John Bonham died of asphyxiation as a result of alcohol consumption, thus initiating the dissolution of the group. *Coda,* a collection of studio outtakes and early recordings, was released in 1982.

In 2003, Jimmy Page went back to the vaults and emerged with the DVD *Led Zeppelin,* a two-disc set more than five-and-a-half hours in length. The set includes blistering performances at Albert Hall in 1970, Madison Square in 1973, Earl's Court in 1975, and Knebworth in 1979. This impressive DVD bears out the staggering power and glory of Led Zeppelin at its vibrant peak. Concurrently, Page released *How the West Was Won,* a three-CD live set culled from two 1972 shows in Los Angeles and Long Beach, California, further testament to Zeppelin's scintillating prowess in concert.

Although it has been criticized as much as it has been lauded, Led Zeppelin is without question the most enduring band in rock history. In Page's own assessment, his greatest achievement has been his "ability to create unexpected melodies and harmonies within a rock 'n' roll framework. As a producer I would like to be remembered as someone who was able to push [the band] to the forefront and capture the multifaceted gem that is Led Zeppelin."

Jimmy Page
© 2004 Bob Gruen/Star File

JIMMY PAGE'S GUITAR STYLE

Jimmy Page's Guitar Style

By Andy Aledort

Pinning down Jimmy Page's guitar style is as difficult as pigeon-holing Led Zeppelin's music. Page's primary interest was *sound*, and he covered a vast terrain stylistically, on both acoustic and electric guitar, in the pursuit of new sonic territory.

Jimmy Page has always maintained that he listened to equal doses of folk, classical, and Indian music along with electric blues, rock, and R&B. Page's electric guitar soloing style finds its roots in the blues work of B.B. King, Otis Rush, Buddy Guy, Hubert Sumlin, Elmore James, Albert King, and Freddie King, as well as the fret-burning rockabilly players Cliff Gallup, Scotty Moore, James Burton, and Paul Burlison.

In the early '60s, Jimmy's guitar of choice was a '50s Les Paul Custom, commonly known as the Black Beauty and "fretless wonder." Unfortunately, this guitar was stolen from Jimmy on one of his earliest Zeppelin tours. Following the lead of American blues and rockabilly guitarists, Page restrung his guitar with lighter strings, allowing him to bend pitches easily and produce a razor-sharp tone: the standard wound G string was replaced with an unwound B string—tuning the unwound B down to G makes the string very slinky and easy to bend. The high E string was then used for a B string, and the high A string from a tenor banjo was used for the high E string. Because this was well before the advent of light strings, the majority of blues and rock guitarists of the day adopted this restringing technique.

In the earliest days of Zeppelin, Page's main axe was a '58 Fender Telecaster; this is the only guitar Page used for *Led Zeppelin I,* along with a 1 x 12 Supro amplifier. By *Zeppelin II,* a '59 Les Paul Standard had become Jimmy's guitar of choice, also favoring a '58 Les Paul Standard (a gift from Joe Walsh) as a backup. For amplification, the mainstay of the backline became 100-watt Marshalls and 4 x 12 cabinets. The Tele was later called back into service for Jimmy's classic "Stairway to Heaven" solo.

Jimmy also liked to intertwine the sound of electric 12-string guitars from early on. "Thank You" and "Living Loving Maid," from *Zeppelin II,* feature a Vox 12; "Stairway to Heaven" and "The Song Remains the Same" were cut with a Fender Electric XII. Other guitars used less frequently include a Fender Stratocaster, heard on "The Crunge" from *Houses of the Holy,* and a customized '60s Danelectro, played primarily in open tunings and used on cuts such as "Kashmir" and "In My Time of Dying."

Jimmy Page also stands apart from his rock-guitar-god peers because of his substantial abilities as an acoustic flat-picking and fingerstyle guitarist. Examples of his mastery of these styles are found throughout the catalog, prime examples being "Babe, I'm Gonna Leave You" and "Black Mountain Side" *(Zeppelin I),* "That's the Way" and "Bron-Y-Aur Stomp" *(Zeppelin III),* "The Battle of Evermore" and "Going to California" *(Zeppelin IV),* "Over The Hills and Far Away" and "The Rain Song" *(Houses of the Holy),* and "Bron-Yr-Aur" and "Black Country Woman" *(Physical Graffiti).* His main axe when playing acoustic guitar was a '71 Martin D-28.

Though Page is acknowledged as an excellent soloist, technical prowess on the guitar was less a fascination for him than for his fellow countrymen and Yardbirds alumni, the proto-metal virtuosi Eric Clapton and Jeff Beck. Page was more interested in the broader picture: the songwriting, the production, the sound, the attitude, and the presentation. So though he did play brilliant solos in Led Zeppelin, the nature of his true contributions on the guitar are more about the way in which he used his guitar technique to produce sounds, textures, emotions, and atmospheres that were as radical as possible.

Page stretched the conventions of guitar sound by using singularly unique recording techniques, such as overdriving the guitar sound through the mixing board and then sending the signal through a Leslie rotating speaker cabinet; this technique is heard to great effect on "How Many More Times" and the "Good Times Bad Times" guitar solo. Another favorite device was the Vox Tone Bender, an early distortion pedal designed by Brit Roger Mayer, who later would design pedals for Jimi Hendrix. Page also liked to set his Vox wah-wah on full treble for some solos, such as "Whole Lotta Love" *(Zeppelin II)* and "Communication Breakdown" *(Zeppelin I).*

Another innovative technique on *Led Zeppelin I*—and pursued to greater effect on *Led Zeppelin II*'s "Whole Lotta Love"—was Page's use of the violin bow on electric guitar, heard on "Dazed and Confused" and "How Many More Times." Page used the violin bow to produce shimmery, sliding otherworldly sound effects, both chordally and with single notes. By the time of 1975's live *The Song Remains the Same,* Jimmy had turned the technique into an art-form, incorporating dense Echo-Plex (an early tape echo device) effects as well as a Theremin, a peculiar invention that produces an array of pitches controlled by the proximity of one's hand to a vertical metal antennae.

Also singular to Jimmy Page's rock approach was the incorporation of altered guitar tunings on acoustic guitar, a prime example being *Zeppelin I*'s "Black Mountain Side." For this track, Jimmy tuned his guitar (low to high) to D A D G A D, commonly referred to as "dad-gad." This same tuning is heard on "Kashmir," from *Physical Graffiti.*

Page also incorporated open tunings along with standard tunings on electric guitar, heard to great effect on the track "Celebration Day" from *Led Zeppelin III,* where he combines open-A tuning (low to high: E A E A C♯ E) with standard tuning. On "Hats Off to (Roy) Harper" *(Zeppelin III),* Page plays slide on acoustic guitar in a low open-C tuning (C G C E G C). Other examples of Page's incorporation of unusual tunings on acoustic guitar can be heard on *Zeppelin III*'s "Friends" (open C6 [low to high]: C A C G C E), reprised on *Physical Graffiti*'s "Bron-Yr-Aur," and on "Bron-Y-Aur Stomp" (open F [low to high]: C F C F A F). Page continued to investigate unusual altered tunings throughout Led Zeppelin's history.

A standout track on *Led Zeppelin II*—and the track most responsible for the prerequisite extended solo guitar break in live rock performance—is the guitar tour-de-force "Heartbreaker," which features a blistering unaccompanied guitar solo in free time. Curiously, the track was complete when Page decided to insert this "free" guitar solo section, so he recorded the solo at a different time in a different studio and spliced it in. This guitar break aptly demonstrates Page's unique approach to soloing, as he combines string pulling behind the nut (2:07–2:14), aggressive double-picking (2:24–2:30), speedy blues licks (2:36–2:42), and pugilistic hard-hitting rhythm guitar (2:49–2:54).

One of Jimmy Page's greatest performances on record with regard to improvised guitar soloing is most certainly *Zeppelin III*'s "Since I've Been Loving You." Through the entire track, Page pulls from his electric blues influences while at once creating something new and original. By the solo's midpoint (3:46 and 4:03), Page instills a modal approach of F Dorian (F G A♭ B♭ C D E♭)/C Aeolian (C D E♭ F G A♭ B♭) that is radically different from that of standard blues improvisation.

Another aspect of his singular approach is with regard to phrasing. Throughout the "Since I've Been Loving You" solo, Page alternates between aligning his phrases squarely with the beat to playing with no rhythmic regimentation whatsoever, improvising with rhythmic as well as melodic freedom as he plays bursts of quickly crammed notes (3:38–3:52) against slower lines and sustained string bends (4:09–4:15).

Page's desire to push the envelope with his sound grew with each release, and *Led Zeppelin IV* is no exception. On the propulsive "Black Dog," Page routed his guitar signal through a direct box and overdrove the microphone preamp in the mixing board; the signal was then sent through two Urie compressors in series, yielding an otherworldly, hard-edged distortion. Another aural innovation that began at the time of *Led Zeppelin III* was Page's use of an Altair Tube Limiter to alter the quality of the recorded sound of his acoustic guitar.

Led Zeppelin's fifth release, *Houses of the Holy,* reveals Page's continued growth as a composer, guitarist, and producer. His fascination with altered guitar tunings can be heard on songs such as "The Rain Song," which featured yet another unusual guitar tuning of (low to high) D G D G C D; on the live *The Song Remains the Same* version, all of the pitches are one whole step higher (low to high): E A E A D E. "Dancing Days" is played with one guitar in open-G tuning (low to high: D G D G B D) and another guitar in standard tuning.

There are a variety of guitar masterworks on *Houses of the Holy,* such as the ambitious "Over the Hills and Far Away," built from equal doses of acoustic and electric guitar virtuosity. Jimmy pushed the stylistic limits of his guitar playing also, as "The Crunge" reveals the James Brown/funk influence and "D'Yer Mak'er" combines '50s pop with Jamaican reggae. He had not, however, abandoned the power of *the riff,* as evidenced by the blistering album closer, "The Ocean."

One of the most guitar-driven albums in the Zeppelin catalog is *Physical Graffiti*; nearly every track overflows with high-spirited, inspired guitar work, such as Jimmy's brilliant rhythm guitar on "Custard Pie," "In My Time of Dying," "The Wanton Song," "Trampled Under Foot," and "Kashmir"; deft soloing on "The Rover" and "Houses of the Holy"; and meticulous overdubbing on "Ten Years Gone."

From '76's *Presence,* Page sites "Achilles Last Stand" and "Tea for One" as favorites. Around ten minutes each, the former offers hard-driving, airtight rhythm guitar combined with intense soloing across a densely complex arrangement; the latter is a combo groover/slow minor blues in the "Since I've Been Loving You" vein, again built from a well-constructed arrangement and fueled by emotionally inspired blues soloing.

In an ultimate assessment of Jimmy Page as a guitarist, Jimmy gets the last word: "I don't really have a [guitar] technique, as such; I think it's harder to come up with fresh ideas, fresh approaches, and a fresh vision."

All Jimmy Page quotes courtesy of Guitar World.

Robert Plant, 6/15/1975
© 2004 Bob Alford/Star File

John Paul Jones, Madison Square Garden, 1973

Plant and Page, 6/15/1975
© 2004 Bob Alford/Star File

Plant and Page, Wembley Arena, 1971
© 2004 Barrie Wentzall/Star File

John Bonham

Good Times Bad Times

Music and Lyrics by
Jimmy Page, John Paul Jones
and John Bonham

20

Good times, bad times, you know I've had my share. Well, my

wom-an left home for a brown-eyed man, but I still don't seem to care.

See additional lyrics

Ad lib vocal:
I know what it means to be alone,
I sure do wish I was at home.
I don't care what the neighbors say,
I'm gonna love you each and every day.
You can feel the beat within my heart.
Realize, sweet babe, we ain't never gonna part.

Chords used in this song:

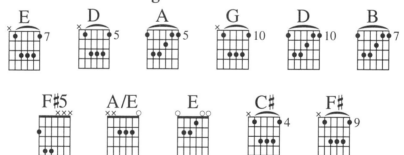

Good Times Bad Times - 3 - 3
FBM0007

YOU SHOOK ME

Words and Music by
Willie Dixon and J.B. Lenoir

Verse 2:
I have a bird that whistles and I have birds that sing.
I have a bird that whistles and I have birds that sing.
I have a bird won't do nothin', oh, oh, buy you a diamond ring.

Verses 3, 4, & 5:
Instrumental solos

Verse 6:
You know you shook me, baby, you shook me all night long.
I said you shook me, baby, you shook me all night long.
You shook me so hard, baby, you shook me all night long.

Chords used in this song:

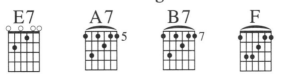

E7   A7   B7   F

FBM0007

Babe, I'm Gonna Leave You

Music and Lyrics by
Anne Bredon, Jimmy Page,
and Robert Plant

Moderately bright, with a half-time feel (♩ = 138)

1. Babe,
2. *See additional lyrics*

ba - by, ba - by,___ I'm gon - na leave you.___ I said ba - by,___ you know___ I'm gon - na leave you. I'll___ leave you when the sum - mer - time,___ leave you when the sum - mer comes a roll - in', leave you when the sum - mer comes a

See additional lyrics for vocal ad lib.

RUBATO

That's when it's call - in' me,____ that's when it's call - in' me____ back____

home.____

Verse 2:
Babe, baby babe, I don't wanna leave you.
I ain't jokin', woman, I got to ramble,
I really got to ramble.
I can hear it callin' me the way it used to do,
I can hear it callin' me back home.

Ad lib. vocal:
I know, I know, I know, I never, I never, I never'll leave you, baby.
But I got to go away from this place, I've got to quit you.
Ooh, baby, baby, baby, baby
Baby, baby, baby, ooh don't you hear it callin'?
Woman, woman, I know, I know it's good to be back again
And I know that one day, baby, it's really gonna grow, yes it is.
Hear what I say, every day.
Baby, it's really growin', you made me happy when skies were grey.
But I've got to go away.
Baby, baby, baby, baby,
That's when it's callin' me,
That's when it's callin' me back home...

Chords used in this song:

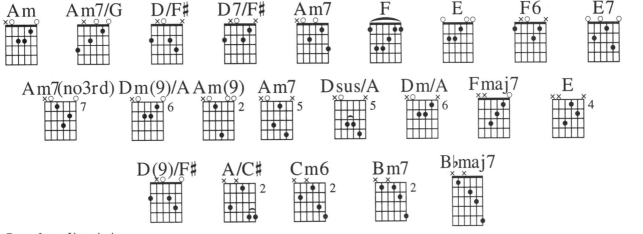

Babe, I'm Gonna Leave You - 4 - 4
FBM0007

DAZED AND CONFUSED

Music and Lyrics by
Jimmy Page

Moderately slow (♩. = 52)

N.C.

Bass Fig.

A VERSE:

1. Been dazed and con-fused_ for so long, it's not true. A-

Bass Fig. Cont.

want-ed a wom - an, nev-er bar-gained for you.____ Lot-sa peo-ple talk-in', few of them know,

soul of a wom-an was cre-at-ed be-low.____ Gtr. & Bass Fig.

2. You hurt____

B VERSE:

_ and a-buse,_ tell-in' all of your lies,_ run 'round,_ sweet ba-by, lord,_ how they hyp-no-tize._

3. 4. *See additional lyrics*

Sweet lit-tle ba-by, I don't know where you been._ Gon-na love you, ba-by, here I come a-gain._

B5

To Coda ✠ | 1.

N.C.   B5   N.C.   B5   N.C.   B5   N.C.

Dazed and Confused - 3 - 1
FBM0007

GUITAR SOLO

Ah._____

D.S. % AL CODA

4. Been dazed and con-

CODA

(GTR. & VOCAL AD LIB.)

Verse 3:
Every day I work so hard, bringin' home my hard-earned pay.
Try to love you, baby, but you push me away.
Don't know where you're goin', only know just where you've been.
Sweet little baby, I want you again.
(To Instrumental Bridge:)

Verse 4:
Been dazed and confused for so long, it's not true.
Wanted a woman, never bargained for you.
Take it easy, baby, let them say what they will.
Tongue wag so much when I send you the bill, oh, yeah, alright.
(To Coda)

Chords used in this song:

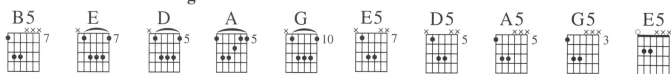

B5   E   D   A   G   E5   D5   A5   G5   E5

I Can't Quit You Baby

WORDS AND MUSIC BY
WILLIE DIXON

Slow Blues (♩ = 50)

Oh,_____ I,_____

1. I can't quit you, babe,_
2.-5. *See additional lyrics*

so I'm gon na put you down_ for a while._

I said

I can't quit you, babe,_

I guess I got to put you down_ for a while._

Said you messed up_ my hap-py home,_

made me mis-treat my on-ly_

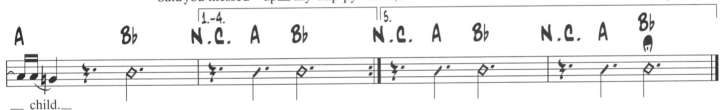

_ child._

Verse 2:
Said you know I love you, baby,
My love for you I could never hide.
Oh, you know I love you, babe,
My love for you I could never hide.
And when I feel you near me, little girl,
I know you are my one desire.

Verses 3 & 4:
Instrumental solo

Verse 5:
When you hear me moanin' and groanin', babe,
You know it hurts me deep down inside.
When you hear me moanin' and groanin', babe,
You know it hurts me deep down inside.
When you hear me holler, baby,
You know you are my one desire.

Chords used in this song:

A

D9

E9

Bb

FBM0007

YOUR TIME IS GONNA COME

MUSIC AND LYRICS BY
JIMMY PAGE AND JOHN PAUL JONES

Ly-in', cheat-in', hurt-in', that's all you seem to do.___
2. *See additional lyrics*

Mess-in' a-round with ev-'ry guy in town,___

put-tin' me down___ for think-in' of some-one new.___

Al-ways the same,___ play-in' your game,___

drive me in-sane,___ trou-ble's gon-na come to you.___

One of these days and it won't be long,_____ you'll look for me but, ba-by, I'll be

gone.___   This is all I got - ta say to you, wom - an.

B Chorus:

Your time is gon - na come.___ Your time is gon - na come.___

Your time is gon - na come.___ Your time is gon - na

1.
come.___

2.
come.___   Your time is gon - na come.___   *Repeat ad lib. and fade*

Verse 2:
Made up my mind to break you this time, won't be so fine, it's my turn to cry.
Do what you want, I won't take the brunt, it's fadin' away, can't feel you anymore.
Don't care what you say 'cause I'm goin' away to stay.
Gonna make you pay for that great big hole in my heart.
People talkin' all around, watch out, woman, no longer is the joke gonna be in my heart,
You been bad to me, woman, but it's comin' back home to you.
(To Chorus:)

Chords used in this song:

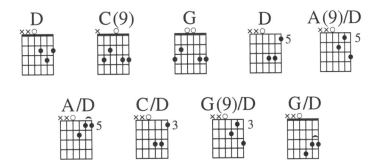

D   C(9)   G   D   A(9)/D

A/D   C/D   G(9)/D   G/D

BLACK MOUNTAIN SIDE

Gtr. tuned:
⑥ = D ③ = G
⑤ = A ② = A
④ = D ① = D

Music by
Jimmy Page

*Recording sounds a half step lower than written.

Black Mountain Side - 2 - 1
FBM0007

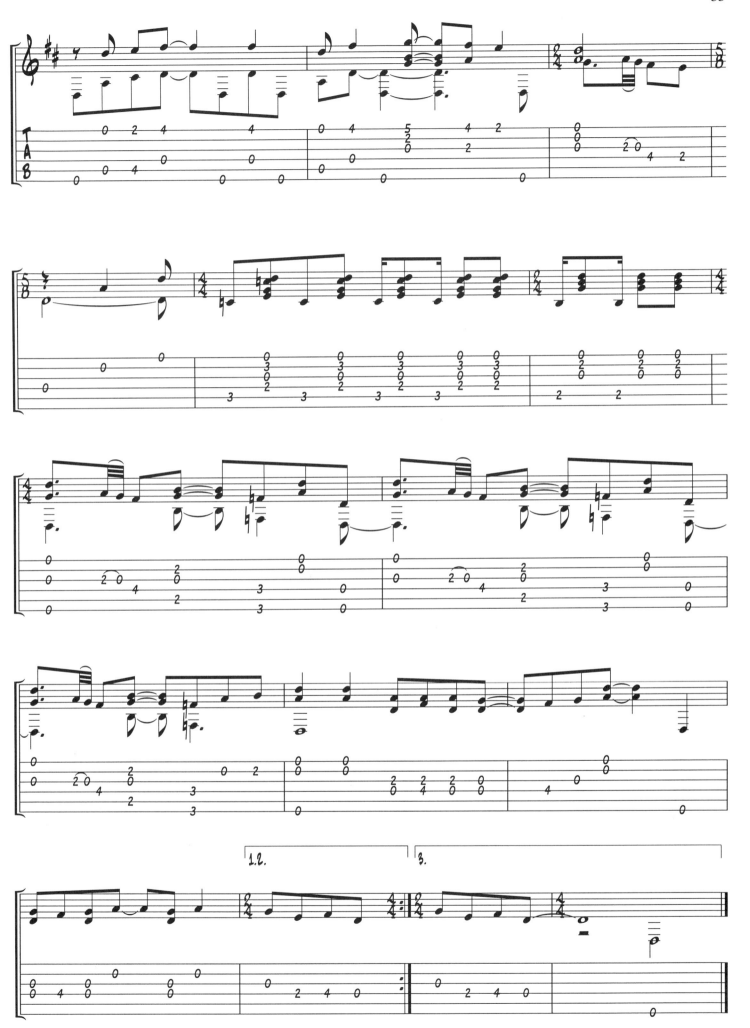

COMMUNICATION BREAKDOWN

Music and Lyrics by
Jimmy Page, John Paul Jones
and John Bonham

1. Hey, girl, stop what you do-in'.
2.3. *See additional lyrics*

Hey, girl, you'll drive me to ru-in.

I don't know what it is I like a-bout you, but I like it a lot.

Oh, let me hold you, let me feel your lov-in' charms.

Com-mu-ni-ca-tion break-down, it's al-ways the same.

I'm hav-ing a ner-vous break-down, drive me in-sane.

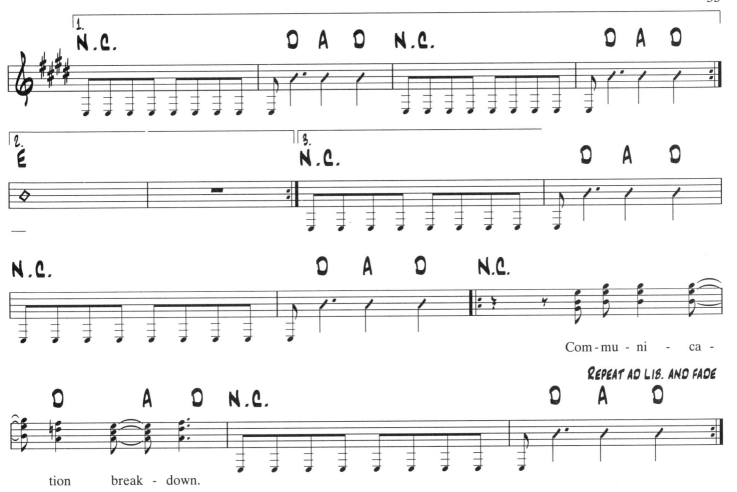

Verse 2:
Hey, girl, I got something I think you ought to know.
Hey, babe, I wanna tell you that I love you so.
I wanna hold you in my arms, yeah!
I'm never gonna let you go,
Yes, I like your charms.
(To Chorus:)

Verse 3:
Guitar solo
(To Chorus:)

Chords used in this song:

HOW MANY MORE TIMES

Music and Lyrics by
Jimmy Page, John Paul Jones
and John Bonham

1. How

A VERSE:
WITH RIFF

man - y more times,____ treat me____ the way you

2. See additional lyrics

wan - na do?____ How

man - y more times,____ treat me the way you wan - na

do?____ When I

give you all my love,____ please,____ please____

__ be true.____

How Many More Times - 5 - 1
FBM0007

2. I'll give you

GUITAR SOLO AD LIB.

See additional lyrics for ad lib. vocals

How Many More Times - 5 - 2
FBM0007

40

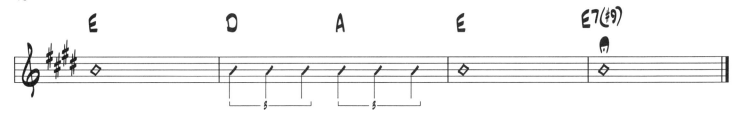

Verse 2:
I'll give you all I've got to give: rings, pearls and all;
I'll give you all I've got to give: rings, pearls and all.
I've got to get you together, baby, I'm sure, sure you're gonna crawl.

Ad lib. vocals 1:
I was a young man, I couldn't resist,
Started thinkin' it over, just what I missed.
Got me a girl and I kissed her and then and then...
Whoops! Oh, Lord, well I did it again.
Now I got ten children on my own.
I got another child on the way, that makes eleven.
But I'm in constant heaven,
I know it's all right in my mind,
I got a little schoolgirl and she's all mine.
I can't get through to her 'cause it doesn't permit.
But I'm gonna give her everything I got to give.

Ad lib. vocals 2:
But I've got to get to you, baby.
Oh, please come home.
I've got to get to you, baby.
Why don't you please come home?
Why don't you please come home?
Why don't you please come home, home?

Chords used in this song:

E   D   A   D/A   E/B   E   E7(♯9)   B   G

WHOLE LOTTA LOVE

Music and Lyrics by
Jimmy Page, Robert Plant,
John Paul Jones and John Bonham

Verse 2:
You've been learnin', and baby, I mean learnin'.
All them good times, baby, baby, I've been yearnin'.
Way, way down inside, honey, you need it.
I'm gonna give you my love.
I'm gonna give you my love.
(To Chorus:)

Verse 3:
You've been coolin', baby, I've been droolin'.
All the good times, baby, I've been misusin'.
Way, way down inside, I'm gonna give you my love.
I'm gonna give you every inch of my love.
Gonna give you my love.
(To Chorus:)

Chords used in this song:

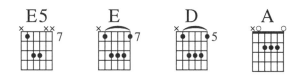

What Is and What Should Never Be

Music and Lyrics by
Jimmy Page and Robert Plant

2. And if you say to me to-

Verse 2:
And if you say to me tomorrow,
Oh, what fun it all would be.
Then what's to stop us, pretty baby
But what is and what should never be.
(To Chorus:)

Verse 3 & Chorus 3:
Instrumental

Verse 4:
So if you wake up with the sunrise
And all your dreams are still as new.
And happiness is what you need so bad,
Girl, the answer lies with you, yeah.
(To Chorus:)

Chords used in this song:

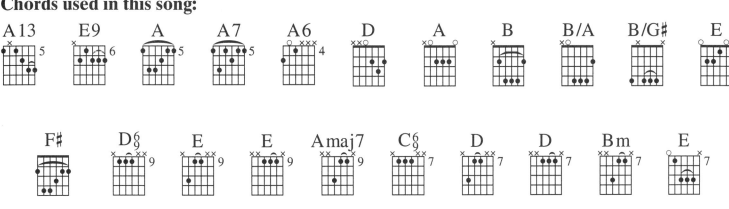

A13   E9   A   A7   A6   D   A   B   B/A   B/G#   E

F#   D⁶/₉   E   E   Amaj7   C⁶/₉   D   D   Bm   E

What Is and What Should Never Be - 2 - 2
FBM0007

THE LEMON SONG

Music and Lyrics by
Jimmy Page, Robert Plant,
John Paul Jones and John Bonham

The Lemon Song - 3 - 1
FBM0007

3. Peo-ple tell me, ba - by, can't be sat - is - fied.___
4. 5. 7. *See additional lyrics*
6. *Guitar solo ad lib.*

The Lemon Song - 3 - 2
FBM0007

Try-in' to wor-ry me, ba - by, but I nev-er end up,   get to be my - self.__

A

Peo-ple wor-ry, ba - by,   to keep you sat - is - fied.__

B   **A**

Ah,   let me tell you, babe,   ah,__ you ain't noth - in' but a   two bit,__ no good__

1. 2. 3. 4.   **5.**   **D.S. % AL CODA**
E   **E**   **TEMPO 2 (♩ = 152)**

__ jive.__

CODA   **B**   **RUBATO**
                    A N.C.   **E7(#9) N.C.**

I'm gon - na leave my__ chil-dren   down on this__ kill-ing   floor.__

Verse 2:
I should have listened, baby, to my second mind.
Oh, I should have listened, baby, to my second mind.
Every time I go away and leave you, darling,
You send me the blues way down the line. Oh!
(To Guitar solo)

Verse 4:
I went to sleep last night, I work as hard as I can.
I bring home my money, you take my money,
Give it to another man.
I should have quit you, baby, oh, such a long time ago, oh.
I wouldn't be here with all my troubles, mm,
Down on this killin' floor.

Verse 5:
Squeeze me, babe, till the juice runs down my leg.
Oh, squeeze, squeeze me, baby,
Till the juice runs down my leg.
The way you squeeze my lemon,
I'm gonna fall right out of bed.
(To Guitar solo ad lib.)

Verse 7:
(Vocal ad libs.)
(To Guitar solo)

Chords used in this song:

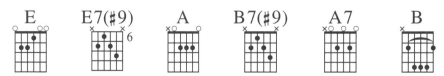

The Lemon Song - 3 - 3
FBM0007

Thank You

Music and Lyrics by
Jimmy Page and Robert Plant

Thank You - 3 - 2
FBM0007

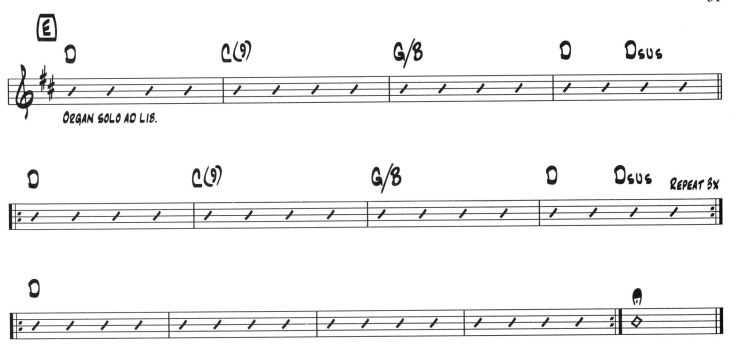

Verse 2:
And so today, my world it smiles,
Your hand in mine, we walk the miles.
But thanks to you it will be done,
For you to me are the only one, ah, yeah.
Happiness, no more be sad,
Happiness, I'm glad.
(To Verse 3:)

Chords used in this song:

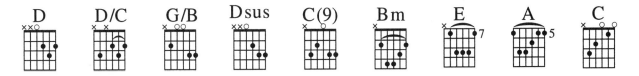

Heartbreaker

Music and Lyrics by
Jimmy Page, Robert Plant,
John Paul Jones and John Bonham

1. Hey, fel-las, have you heard the news,— you know that An-nie's back— in town.— It
2.3. *See additional lyrics*

won't take long, just watch and see all the fel-las lay their mon-ey down.— Her

style is new— but the face's the same— as it was so long a-go.— But

from her eyes— a dif-'rent smile— like that of one who know.—

Heartbreaker - 3 - 1
FBM0007

54

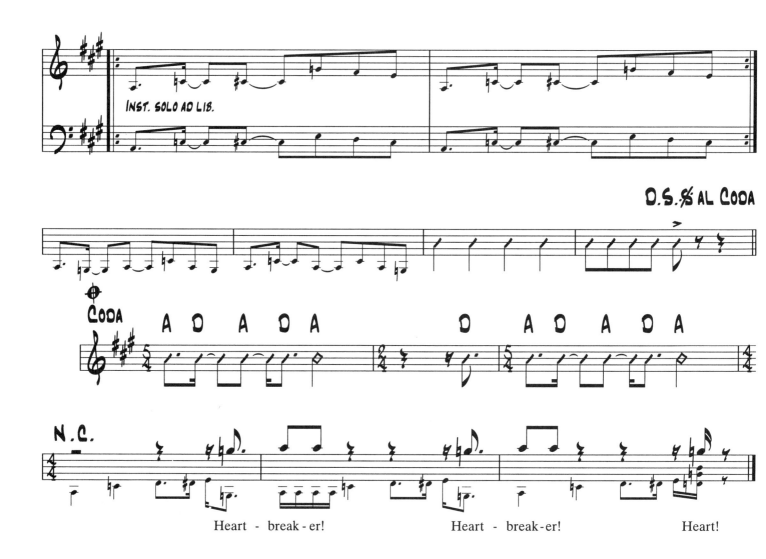

Heart - break - er!   Heart - break-er!   Heart!

Verse 2:
Well, it's been ten years and maybe more since I first set eyes on you.
The best years of my life gone by. Here I am alone and blue.
Some people cry and some people die by the wicked ways of love.
But I'll just keep rollin' along with the grace of the Lord above.

Verse 3:
Work so hard I can't unwind, get some money saved,
Abuse my love a thousand times, however hard I try.
Heartbreaker, your time has come, can't take your evil ways.
Go away, you heartbreaker.

Chords used in this song:

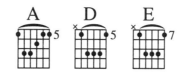

Living Loving Maid
(She's Just A Woman)

Music and Lyrics by
Jimmy Page and Robert Plant

Fast Rock (♩ = 152)

A Verses 1 & 3:

1. With a pur-ple um-ber-el-la and a fif-ty cent hat,___
3. See additional lyrics

(Liv-in', lov-in',

mis-sus cool rides out___ in her aged___ Cad-il-lac.
she's just a wom-an.)

(Liv-in', lov-in',

B Chorus:

she's just a wom-an.) Come on, babe,___ on the round a-bout,
2x - Guitar solo ad lib.

ride on the mer-ry-go-round.___ We all know___ what your

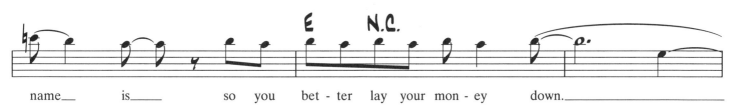

name___ is___ so you bet-ter lay your mon-ey down.___

2. Al - i - mo - ny, al - i - mo - ny pay - in' your__ bills. (Liv - in', lov - in',
4. *See additional lyrics*

When your con - science hits,____ you knock it
she's just a wom - an.)

back with pills.__ (Liv - in', lov - in', she's just a wom - an.)

Come on, babe,__ on the round a - bout, ride on the mer - ry - go - round.__

_____ We all know__ what your name__ is____ so you

bet - ter lay your mon - ey down._____

Living Loving Maid - 3 - 2
FBM0007

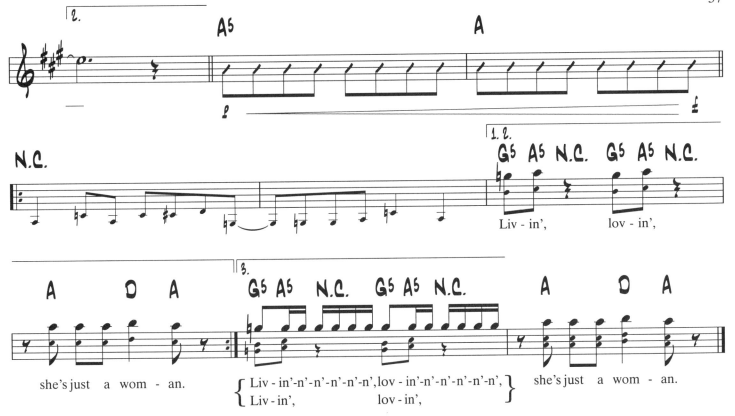

shes just a woman.

Liv - in', lov - in',

{ Liv - in'-n'-n'-n'-n'-n', lov - in'-n'-n'-n'-n'-n', }
{ Liv - in', lov - in', }

she's just a wom - an.

Verse 3:
Tellin' tall tales of how it used to be,
(Livin', lovin', she's just a woman.)
With the butler and the maid and the servants three.
(Livin', lovin', she's just a woman.)
(To Guitar solo)

Verse 4:
Nobody hears a single word you say,
(Livin', lovin', she's just a woman.)
But you keep on talkin' 'til your dyin' day.
(Livin', lovin', she's just a woman.)
(To Chorus:)

Chords used in this song:

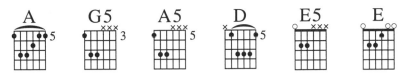

Living Loving Maid - 3 - 3
FBM0007

Ramble On

Music and Lyrics by
Jimmy Page and Robert Plant

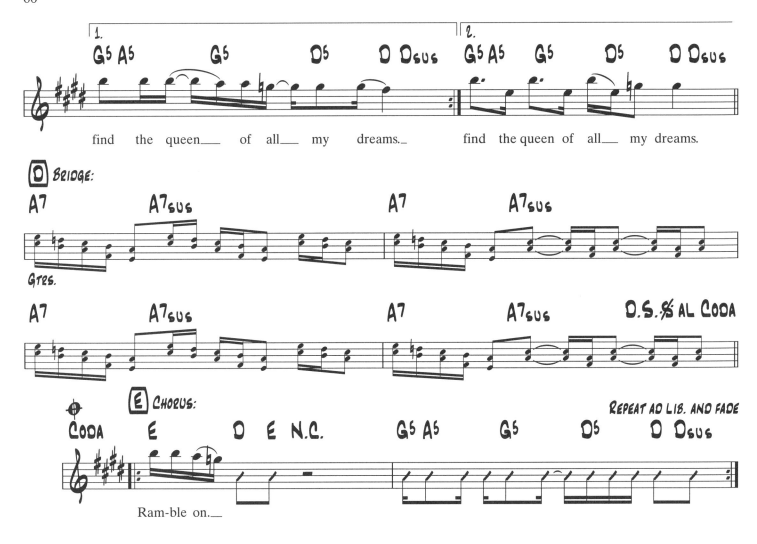

find the queen___ of all___ my dreams.___   find the queen of all___ my dreams.

D BRIDGE:

Gtrs.

D.S. ⅋ AL CODA

E CHORUS:

CODA

Ram-ble on.___

REPEAT AD LIB. AND FADE

Verse 2:
Got no time to for spreadin' roots,
The time has come to be gone.
And though our health we drank a thousand times,
It's time to ramble on.
(To Guitar solo)

Verse 3:
Mine's a tale that can't be told,
My freedom I hold dear.
How years ago in days of old,
When magic filled the air.
T'was in the darkest depths of Mordor,
I met a girl so fair.
But Gollum, and the evil one,
Crept up and slipped away with her, her, her, her, her, yeah,
There ain't nothing I can do, no.
I guess I'll keep on...
(To Coda)

Chords used in this song:

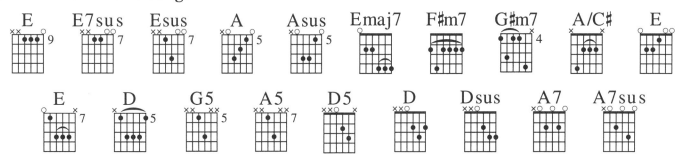

Bring It On Home

WORDS AND MUSIC BY
WILLIE DIXON AND J.B. LENOIR

62

63

Bring it on home,— bring it on home to you.—

Bridge 2:
Went a little walk downtown,
Messed and got back late.
Found a note there waiting,
It said, "Daddy, I just can't wait."
Bring it on home, *etc.*

Bridge 3:
Tell you, pretty baby,
You love to mess me 'round.
I'm gonna give you lovin', baby.
Gonna move you out o' town.
Bring it on home, *etc.*

Bridge 4:
Sweetest little baby
Daddy ever saw.
I'm gonna give you lovin',
I'm gonna give you more.
Bring it on home, *etc.*

Chords used in this song:

E   B   A   E7   A/E   E5

Bring It on Home - 3 - 3
FBM0007

Gtr. tuned in Drop D:
⑥ = D ③ = G
⑤ = A ② = B
④ = D ① = E

Moby Dick

Music by
Jimmy Page, John Bonham
and John Paul Jones

A Moderately (♩ = 96)
N.C.

(GTR. FILLS)

(GTR. FILLS)   (GTR. FILLS)

(GTR. FILLS)

Moby Dick - 2 - 1
FBM0007

Chords used in this song:

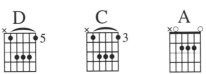

Gtr. tuned in Open C:
⑥ = C ③ = G
⑤ = G ② = C
④ = C ① = E

FRIENDS

MUSIC AND LYRICS BY
JIMMY PAGE AND ROBERT PLANT

MODERATE FOLK ROCK (♩ = 80) (♫ = ♪³♪)

ACOUS. GTR.

C/Eb C/D C/F C/E C/G C/F#

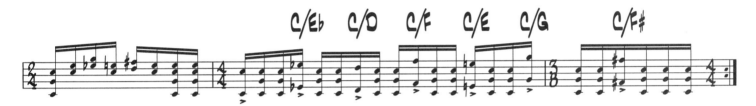

A VERSE:
C   C/G   C/F#   C/G

1. Bright light al - most blind - ing, black night still there shin - ing,
2. *See additional lyrics*

C/A   C/E   C/F#   C/Db

I can't stop, keep on climb - ing, look-ing for what I knew.

C   C/G   C/F#   C/G

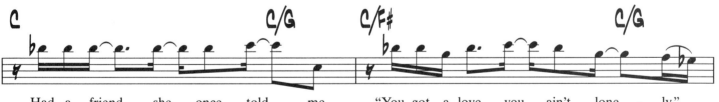

Had a friend, she once told me, "You got a love, you ain't lone - ly."

C/A   C/E   C/F#   C/Db

Now she's gone and left me on - ly look-ing for what I knew.

Friends - 3 - 1
FBM0007

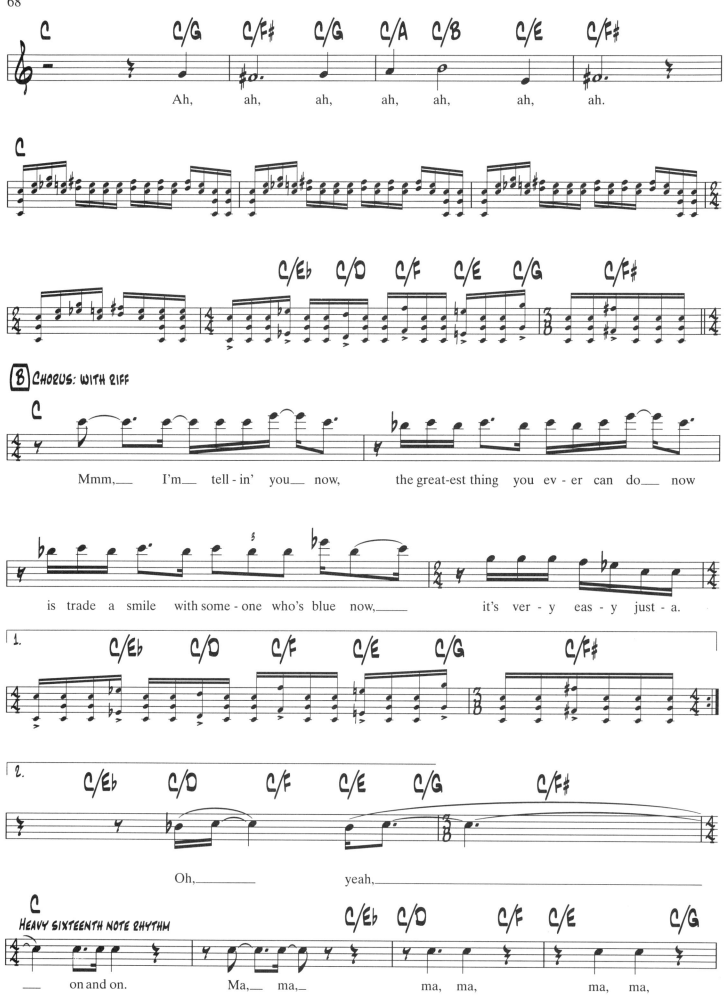

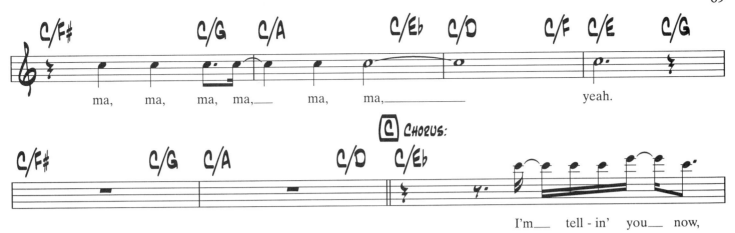

ma, ma, ma, ma, ma, ma, yeah.

Ⓒ CHORUS:

I'm tell-in' you now,

the great-est thing you ev-er can do now   is trade a smile with some-one who's blue now,

Sixteenth notes straighten out, slightly faster

it's ver-y eas-y,   it's ver-y eas-y,   it's ver-y eas-y,   it's eas-y,

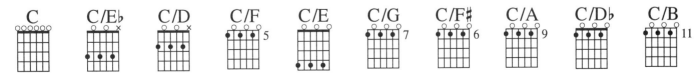

ease   yeah, yeah, yeah.

Verse 2:
Met a man on the roadside crying,
Without a friend there's no denying,
You're incomplete, there'll be no finding,
Looking for what you knew.
So anytime somebody needs ya,
Don't let them down, although it grieves ya.
Some day you'll need someone like they do,
Looking for what you knew.
Ah, ah, ah, ah, ah, ah, ah.
(To Chorus:)

Chords used in this song:

C C/Eb C/D C/F C/E C/G C/F# C/A C/Db C/B

Friends - 3 - 3
FBM0007

IMMIGRANT SONG

Music and Lyrics by
Jimmy Page and Robert Plant

west-ern___ shore.___

(RIFF CONT.)

Ah,_____ ah._____

2. We ___ So

now you'd bet-ter stop___ and re-build__ all your ru-ins, for peace and trust can__ win the day de-

spite of all your__ los - ing.___

Ooh,___ ooh,___ ooh.___ Ooh,___ ooh,___ ooh.___

Chords used in this song:

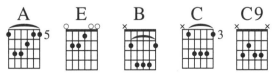

Celebration Day

Music and Lyrics by
Jimmy Page, Robert Plant
and John Paul Jones

1. Her face is cracked from smil-ing, all the fears that she's been hid-ing,
3. 5. *See additional lyrics*

and it seems that pret-ty soon ev-'ry-bod-y's gon-na know.

2. And her voice is sore from shout-ing, cheer-ing
4. 6. *See additional lyrics*

win-ners who are los-ing, and she wor-ries if their days are few and soon they'll have to

go.

* Opt. Tune 1 guitar: ⑥ = A

Celebration Day - 3 - 1

FBM0007

73

74

REPEAT AD LIB. AND FADE

__ yeah.   You're gone,__   yeah.   Bye, bye, bye, bye, bye.

Verse 3:
She hears them talk of new ways
To protect the home she lives in,
Then she wonders what it's all about
When they break down the door.

Verse 4:
Her name is Brown or White or Black,
You know her very well.
You hear her cries of mercy
As the winners toll the bell.
(To Chorus:)

Verse 5:
Oh, there is a train that leaves the station
Heading for your destination,
But the price you pay to nowhere
Has increased a dollar more.
Spoken: Yes, it has.

Verse 6:
And if you walk you're gonna get there
Though it takes a little longer,
And when you see it in the distance
You will wring your hands and moan.
Oh, yeah, and moan.
(To Coda)

Chords used in this song:

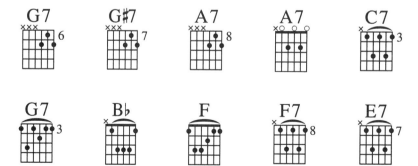

Celebration Day - 3 - 3
FBM0007

Out on the Tiles

Music and Lyrics by
Jimmy Page, Robert Plant
and John Bonham

Verse 3:
I'm so glad I'm living, gonna tell the world I am,
Got me a fine woman, she says that I'm her man.
One thing that I know for sure gonna give her all the lovin'
Like nobody, nobody, nobody, nobody can.

Verse 4:
Standing in the noon-day sun, tryin' to flag a ride,
People go and people come, see my rider right by my side.
It's a total disgrace, they set the pace, it must be a race,
The best thing I can do is run.
(To Chorus:)

Chords used in this song:

Since I've Been Loving You

Music and Lyrics by
Jimmy Page, Robert Plant
and John Paul Jones

79

Said I've been cry-in', yeah, yeah.   Oh, my tears, they fell like rain.

Don't you hear,   don't you hear them fall-ing?   Don't you hear,   don't you hear them fall - ing?

Ah,_____ yeah.   Since I've been lov-in',   I'm gon - na lose   my wor-ried

mind.__

Verse 2:
Everybody trying to tell me
That you didn't mean me no good.
I've been trying, Lord, let me tell you.
Let me tell you I really did the best I could.
I've been working from seven to eleven every night.
It kinda makes my life a drag.
Lord, you know it ain't right.
Since I've been loving you,
I'm about to lose my worried mind.

Verse 3:
Guitar solo ad lib.

Verse 4:
Do you remember, mama, when I knocked upon your door?
I said you had the nerve to tell me you didn't want me no more.
I open my front door, hearing my back door slam.
You must have one of them new-fangled back door man.
I've been working from seven to eleven every night.
It kinda makes my life a drag.
Ah, yeah, it makes it a drag.
Baby, since I've been loving you,
I'm about to lose my worried mind.

Chords used in this song:

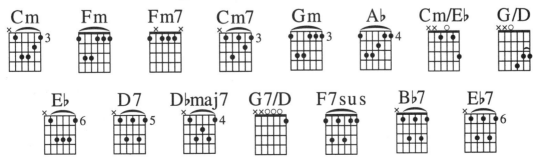

Since I've Been Loving You - 2 - 2
FBM0007

Gallows Pole

Traditional
Arrangement By
Jimmy Page and Robert Plant

Country Folk Rock Ballad (♩ = 100)

Verse 2:
I couldn't get no silver,
I couldn't get no gold.
You know that we're too damn poor
To keep you from the gallows pole.
(To Chorus 2:)

Verse 4:
Brother, I brought you some silver, yeah,
I brought a little gold,
I brought a little of everything
Keep you from the gallows pole.
Yes, I brought you, keep you from the gallows pole.
(To Chorus 3:)

Verse 5:
Sister, I implore you, take him by the hand.
Take him to some shady bower,
Save me from the wrath of this man.
Please take him,
Save me from the wrath of this mad man.

Chorus 4:
Hangman, hangman, upon your face a smile.
Tell me that I'm free to ride,
Ride for many mile, mile, mile.

Verse 7:
Brother brought me silver,
And your sister warmed my soul,
But now I laugh and pull so hard,
See ya swinging on the gallows pole, yeah.
But now I laugh and pull so hard,
See ya swinging on the gallows pole, pole, pole.

Chords used in this song:

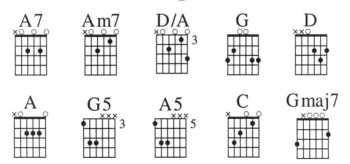

Tangerine

Music and Lyrics by
Jimmy Page

*To match original recording, tune all guitars down 1/2 step.

Tangerine - 3 - 1
FBM0007

and now a thou-sand years___ be-tween._____

2. Think-ing how it used to be, does she still re-mem-ber times like

these? To think of us a-gain? And I do._

86

be - tween.

ELEC. GTR. SOLO AD LIB.

12-STRING GTR.

Chords used in this song:

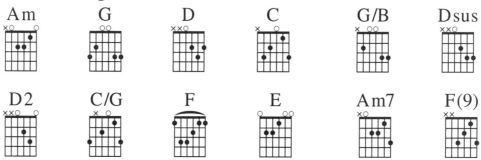

That's The Way

Music and Lyrics by
Jimmy Page and Robert Plant

Gtr. tuned in Open G:
⑥ = D   ③ = G
⑤ = G   ② = B
④ = D   ① = D

Verses 1, 2, 4, & 5:

1. I don't know how I'm gon - na tell you   I can't play with you no
2.4.5. See additional lyrics

more.   I don't know how I'm gon - na do what ma - ma told me,

my friend,_ the boy next door.

*Original recording in G♭.

That's the Way - 3 - 1
FBM0007

That's the Way - 3 - 2
FBM0007

ma-ma said__ that's the way it's gon-na stay,_____ yeah.__

Ah,__ ah,__ ah,_____ ah._____

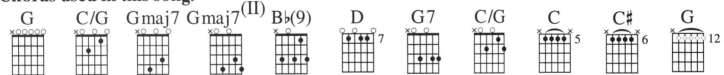

Verse 2:
I can't believe what people saying,
You're gonna let your hair hang down.
I'm satisfied to sit here working all day long,
You're in the darkest side of town.

Verse 4:
And yesterday I saw you standing by the river,
And weren't those tears that filled your eyes?
And all the fish that lay in dirty water dying,
Had they got you hypnotized?

Verse 5:
And yesterday I saw you kissing tiny flowers,
But all that lives is born to die.
And so I say to you that nothing really matters,
And all you do is stand and cry.

Verse 6:
I don't know what to say about it,
When all your ears have turned away.
But now's the time to look and look again at what you see,
Is this the way it ought to stay?
(To Chorus:)

Chords used in this song:

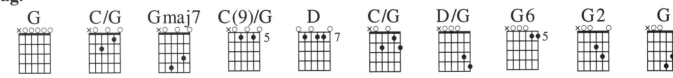

Tag:

That's the Way - 3 - 3
FBM0007

BRON-Y-AUR STOMP

Music and Lyrics by
Jimmy Page, Robert Plant
and John Paul Jones

Gtr. tuned in Open D:
⑥ = D ③ = F#
⑤ = A ② = A
④ = D ① = D
Capoed at 3 fr.

PLAY 3X

Come on now,__ well, let me tell__ you, what you're miss-

ing mess-ing 'round them brick walls.__

Verse 2:
Well, if the sun shines so bright,
Or our way is darkest night,
The road we choose is always right, so fine.
Ah, can a love be so strong
When so many loves go wrong?
Will our love go on and on and on and on and on.
(To Chorus:)

Verse 3:
So of one thing I am sure,
It's a friendship so pure,
Angels singing all around my door so fine.
Yeah, ain't but one thing to do,
Spend my natural life with you,
You're the finest dog I knew, so fine.

Chorus 3:
When you're old and your eyes are dim.
There ain't no old shep gonna happen again.
We'll still go walking down country lanes,
I'll sing the same old song, hear me call your name.

Chords used in this song:

All chords are capo 3. All fret numbers are counted from the capo.

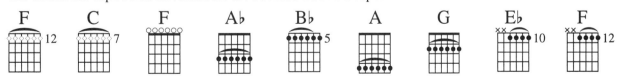

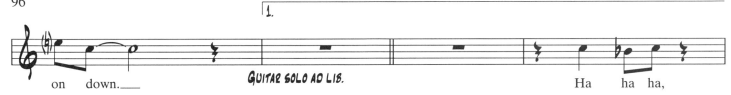

on down.____   *GUITAR SOLO AD LIB.*   Ha   ha   ha,

ha   ha   ha ha,   ha   ha   ha ha,   ha   ha   ha ha,   ha   ha   ha ha.____

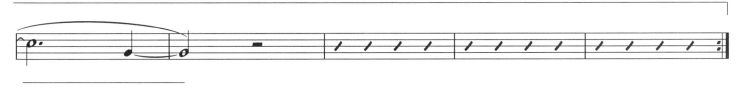

GUITAR SOLO AD LIB.   *D.S. ℅ AL CODA*

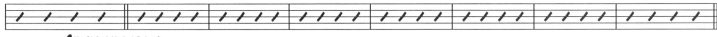

GUITAR SOLO AD LIB.

⊕ **CODA**

GUITAR SOLO AD LIB.   *RIT.*   *FADE:*

Verse 3:
Listen, mama, put on your morning gown.
Put on your nightshirt, mama,
We gonna shake 'em down, yeah.
Must I holler? Must I, must I,
Must I shake 'em on down?

Refrain:
Ooh well, I've done been mistreated, babe,
But hey, I believe I'll shake 'em on down.
(To Guitar solo)

Verse 4:
Gave my baby twenty dollar bill.
If that don't fetch her
I'm sure my shot, shot, shotgun will.
Yeah, I gave my babe twenty dollar bill.
Well, if that don't get that woman,
I'm, I'm sure my shotgun will.
Gonna go shoot her now.
(To Coda)

Chords used in this song:

C   E♭   C(II)   F   G

Black Dog

Music and Lyrics by
Jimmy Page, Robert Plant
and John Paul Jones

* VOCAL SUNG 1 OCTAVE HIGHER.

Black Dog - 3 - 1
FBM0007

Verse 3:
Didn't take too long 'fore I found out what
People mean by down and out.

Spent my money, took my car,
Started tellin' her friends she gonna be a star.

I don't know, but I been told,
A big-legged woman ain't got no soul.
(To Chorus:)

Verse 4:
All I ask for, all I pray,
Steady loaded woman gonna come my way.

Need a woman gonna hold my hand
Will tell me no lies, make me a happy man.
Ah ah ah ah ah ah ah ah ah ah ah ah ah.
(To Coda)

Chords used in this song:

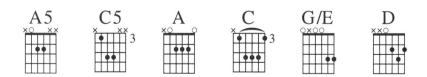

Rock and Roll

Music and Lyrics by
Jimmy Page, Robert Plant,
John Paul Jones and John Bonham

get it back, let me get it back, mm ba - by, where I_____ come

A

from._____

It's been a long time, been a long time, been a long,

N.C.

lone - ly, lone - ly, lone - ly, lone - ly, lone - ly time.

1.3. **A**

Yes, it has._____

2. It's

2. **A**

time.

Oh._____

D.S. %

4. **A**

time.

B Outro:

Yeah,_____ hey. Yeah,_____ hey.

With Gtr. Fig.

Rock and Roll - 3 - 2

FBM0007

Yeah,___ hey. Yeah,___ hey.

Ooh, yeah, ooh,__ yeah._ Ooh, yeah, ooh,__ yeah._ It's

been a long time, been a long time, been a long, lone - ly, lone - ly, lone -

ly, lone - ly, lone - ly time. (DRUM FILL)

Verse 2:
It's been a long time since the book of love.
I can't count the tears of a life with no love.
A-carry me back, carry me back, carry me back,
Mm-baby, where I come from, whoa-whoa, whoa-oh-oh-ho.
It's been a long time, been a long time,
Been a long, lonely, lonely, lonely, lonely, lonely time.
Ah, ah-ah, ah-ah.
(To Guitar solo)

Verse 4:
Oh, it seems so long since we walked in the moonlight
A-makin' vows that just couldn't work right.
Haw, yeah, open your arms, open your arms, open your arms,
Baby, let my love come running in, a-yeah.
It's been a long time, been a long time,
Been a long, lonely, lonely, lonely, lonely, lonely time.
(To Outro:)

Chords used in this song:

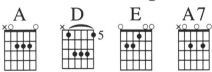

THE BATTLE OF EVERMORE

Dark Lord rides in force to-night, and time will tell us all. Oh,
ing light.

throw down your plow and hoe, rest not to lock your homes.

Side by side we wait the might of the dark - est of them all. Oh.

Ah.

B CHORUS:

1. I hear horses' thun - der down in the val - ley be - low.
2. 3. *See additional lyrics*

I'm wait - ing for the An-gels of Av - a-lon, wait-ing for the east - ern glow. 2.3. The

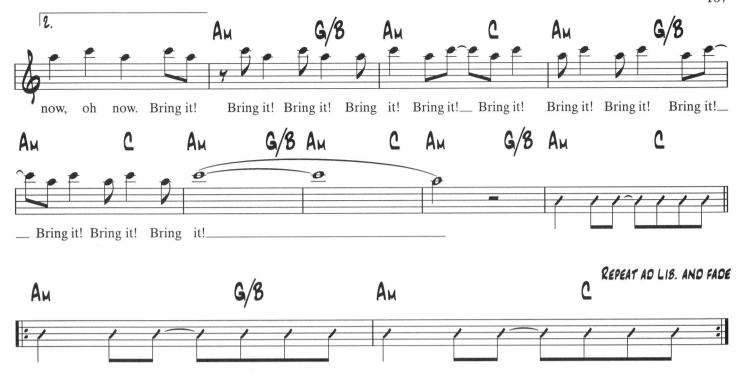

now, oh now. Bring it! Bring it! Bring it! Bring it! Bring it!__ Bring it! Bring it! Bring it! Bring it!__

__ Bring it! Bring it! Bring it!_____

REPEAT AD LIB. AND FADE

Verse 2:
(Male voice:)
The apples of the valley hold,
The seas of happiness.
The ground is rich from tender care,
Repay, do not forget, no, no.
(Female voice:)
Oh, dance in the dark of night,
Sing to the morning light.
(Male voice:)
The apples turn to brown and black,
The tyrant's face is red.
(Female voice:)
Oh, war is the common cry,
Pick up your swords and fly.
(Male voice:)
The sky is filled with good and bad
That mortals never know.

Chorus 2:
Oh, well, the night is long,
The beads of time pass slow.
Tired eyes on the sunrise,
Waiting for the Eastern glow.

Verse 3:
(Male voice:)
The pain of war cannot exceed
The woe of aftermath.
The drums will shake the castle wall,
The Ring Wraiths ride in black.
Ride on.
(Female voice:)
Ah, sing as you raise your bow,
Shoot straighter than before.
(Male voice:)
No comfort has the fire at night
That lights the face so cold.
(Female voice:)
Oh, dance in the dark of night,
Sing to the morning light.
(Male voice:)
The magic runes are writ in gold
To bring the balance back.

Chorus 3:
At last the sun is shining,
The clouds of blue roll by.
With flames from the dragon of darkness,
The sunlight blinds his eyes.
(To Bridge:)

Chords used in this song:

 Am G/B C D Am7 G7

Stairway to Heaven

Music and Lyrics by
Jimmy Page and Robert Plant

1. There's a

110

Stairway to Heaven - 5 - 3
FBM0007

112

Chords used in this song:

Stairway to Heaven - 5 - 5
FBM0007

Misty Mountain Hop

Music and Lyrics by
Jimmy Page, Robert Plant
and John Paul Jones

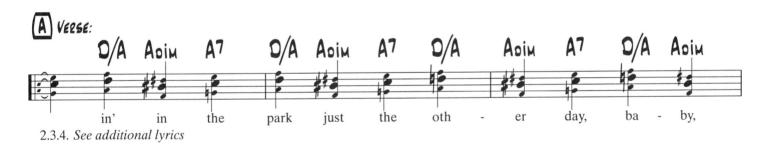

in' in the park just the oth - er day, ba - by,

2.3.4. *See additional lyrics*

what do you, what do you think I saw?____

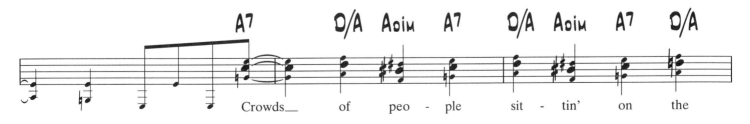

Crowds____ of peo - ple sit - tin' on the

114

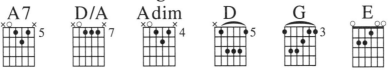

Verse 2:
I didn't notice but it had got very dark and I was really,
Really out of my mind.
Just then a policeman stepped up to me and asked us,
Said please, hey, would we care to all get in line.
Get in line.
(Spoken:) Well, you know.

Chorus 2:
They asked us to stay for tea
And have some fun, woh, oh.
He said that his friends would all drop by, ooh.

Verse 3:
Why don't you take a good look at yourself
And describe what you see,
And baby, baby, baby, do you like it?
There you sit, sitting spare like a book on a shelf rustin',
Ah, not trying to fight it.

Chorus 3:
You really don't care if they're comin', woh, oh.
I know that it's all a state of mind, ooh.
(To Instrumental Bridge:)

Verse 4:
If you go down in the streets today, baby, you better,
You better open your eyes.
Folk down there really don't care,
Really don't care, don't care, really don't,
Which, which way the pressure lies.
So I've decided what I'm gonna do now.

Chorus 4:
So I'm packing my bags for the Misty Mountains
Where the spirits go now.
Over the hills where the spirits fly, ooh.
(To Outro:)

Chords used in this song:

A7   D/A   Adim   D   G   E

Misty Mountain Hop - 3 - 3
FBM0007

Four Sticks

Music and Lyrics by
Jimmy Page and Robert Plant

*Chord names reflect guitar voicing—bass plays an "A" pedal point.

Four Sticks - 4 - 2
FBM0007

118

119

Verse 2:
Oh, baby, the river's red,
Aw, baby, in my head.
There's a funny feeling goin' on,
I don't think I can hold out long.
(To Chorus:)

Verse 3:
Craze, baby, mm, the rainbow's end.
Mm, baby, it's just a den for those who hide,
Hide their loves to depths of life
And ruin dreams that we all knew so, babe.
(To Chorus:)

Chords used in this song:

A5 G5 A9 A9/G A9/B A9/C#

A9/F# A9/E G/A B7/A A(9)

Four Sticks - 4 - 4
FBM0007

WHEN THE LEVEE BREAKS

Gtr. tuned in Open F:
⑥ = C ③ = F
⑤ = F ② = A
④ = C ① = C

Music and Lyrics by
Jimmy Page, Robert Plant,
John Paul Jones, John Bonham and Memphis Minnie

Moderate Delta Blues (♩ = 138)

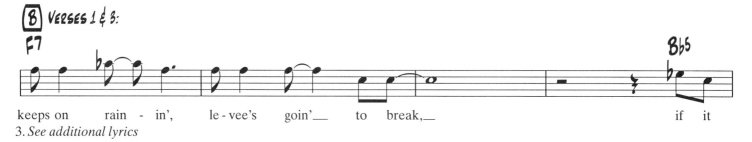

keeps on rain-in', le-vee's goin'___ to break,___   if it
3. *See additional lyrics*

keeps on rain-in', le-vee's goin'___ to break.___   When the

le-vee breaks,___ have no place___ to stay._____

*/Chords-bass function.

Chi - ca - go,_____ goin'_____ to Chi - ca - go,_____

sor - ry but I can't take_____ you. Ah,_____ go - in' down, I'm go - in'

down now. Go - in' down,_____ I'm go - in' down now. Go - in' down, go - in'

down, go - in' down, go - in' down.

REPEAT AD LIB. AND FADE

CONT. VOCAL AD LIBS.

Verse 3:
Cryin' won't help ya', prayin' won't do ya' no good, no,
Cryin' won't help ya', prayin' won't do ya' no good.
Ah, when the levee breaks, mama, you got to move,
Ah, ooo, ooo.

Verse 4:
All last night sat on the levee and moaned,
All last night sat on the levee and moaned.
I'm thinkin' 'bout my baby and my happy home.
(To Coda)

Chords used in this song:

GOING TO CALIFORNIA

Music and Lyrics by
Jimmy Page and Robert Plant

I think I might be sink - in'.

Please throw me a line,_____ if I reach_____ it in time,_ meet you up there_ where the path_____ runs_ straight_ and high._____

D.S. ⅍ AL CODA

CODA

1.

2.

REPEAT AD LIB. AND FADE

(DISTANT CHOIR) Ah_____ ah_____ ah_____ ah.

Verse 3:
Find a queen without a king,
They say she plays guitar and cries and sings, la-la-la-la.
Ride a white mare in the footsteps of dawn,
Tryin' to find a woman who's never, never, never been born.
Standin' on a hill in the mountain of dreams,
Tellin' myself it's not as hard, hard, hard as it seems.
Mm-mm, now.
(To Coda)

Chords used in this song:

D5 G Gmaj7 G6 G^{II} D D2 Dm G/B Dm/A A7

The Song Remains the Same

Moderately Fast Rock (♩ = 144)

Music and Lyrics by
Jimmy Page and Robert Plant

* Bass alternates between A and D for this pattern.

The Song Remains the Same - 5 - 1
FBM0007

The Song Remains the Same - 5 - 2
FBM0007

130

The Song Remains the Same - 5 - 3
FBM0007

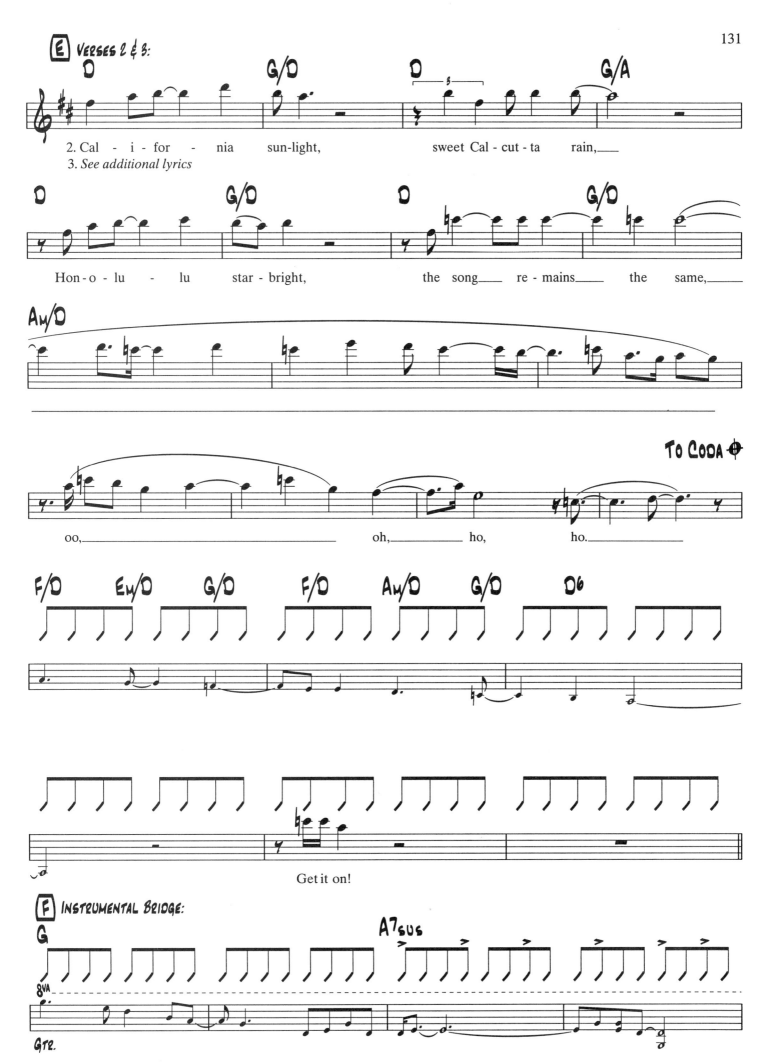

The Song Remains the Same - 5 - 4
FBM0007

Verse 3:
Sing out Hare Hare,
Dance the Hoochie Koo.
City lights are oh so bright,
As we go sliding, sliding, sliding...
(To Coda)

Chords used in this song:

The Song Remains the Same - 5 - 5
FBM0007

THE RAIN SONG

Gtr. tuned:
⑥ = D ③ = G
⑤ = G ② = C
④ = C ① = D

Music and Lyrics by
Jimmy Page and Robert Plant

1. It is the spring-time__ of my lov-ing, the sec-ond__ sea-son__
2. Instrumental
3. See additional lyrics

__ I am to know._____ You are the sun-light in my grow-ing,

so lit-tle warmth__ I__ felt be-fore._____ It is-n't hard to feel me

134

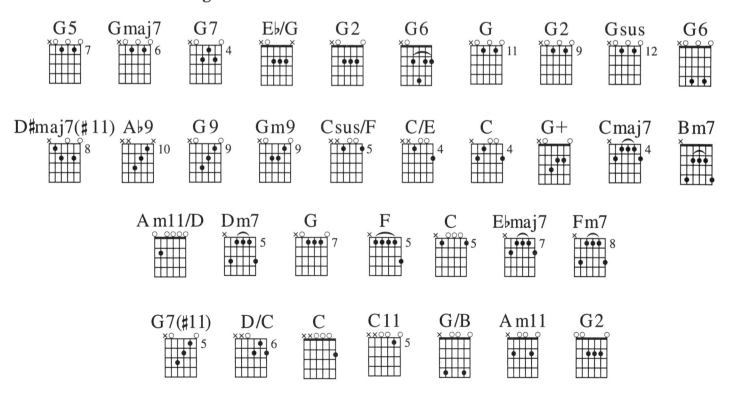

Verse 3:
It is the summer of my smiles,
Flee from me, keepers of the gloom.
Speak to me only with your eyes,
It is to you I give this tune.
It ain't so hard to recognize, oh,
These things are clear to all from time to time.
Hoo. Oh, oh, oh.
(To Bridge:)

Chords used in this song:

G5 Gmaj7 G7 E♭/G G2 G6 G G2 Gsus G6

D#maj7(#11) A♭9 G9 Gm9 Csus/F C/E C G+ Cmaj7 Bm7

Am11/D Dm7 G F C E♭maj7 Fm7

G7(#11) D/C C C11 G/B Am11 G2

Over the Hills and Far Away

Music and Lyrics by
Jimmy Page and Robert Plant

Moderately (♩ = 92)

Dear la-dy, you got the love I need,_ may-be more than e-nough._ Oh, dar-lin', dar-lin', dar-lin', walk a while_ with me._

Oh,_____ you got so__ much,_____ so much,_

Over the Hills and Far Away - 4 - 2
FBM0007

140

Mel - low   is____ the   man____   who   knows   what   he's   been   miss-ing.

Man - y,   man - y   men____   can't   see   the   o - pen   road.____

Over the Hills and Far Away - 4 - 3
FBM0007

Man - y is____ a word that on - ly leaves you guess - in', a - guess - in' 'bout a thing you real - ly ought to know,____

you real - ly ought to know._

DIM.

I real - ly ought to know.____

F

RIT.

Chords used in this song:

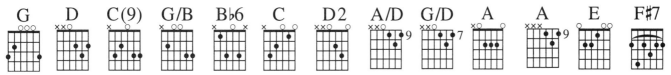

G D C(9) G/B Bb6 C D2 A/D G/D A A E F#7

The Crunge

Music and Lyrics by
Jimmy Page, Robert Plant,
John Paul Jones and John Bonham

1. I wan-na tell you 'bout my good thing.

I ain't dis-clos-in' no names but he sure is a good friend.

I ain't, I ain't gon-na tell you where he comes from but if I tell you you

I'm just try-in' to find_ the bridge.___ Has an-y-bod-y seen_ the

bridge? Please! (Spoken:) Have you seen

the bridge? I ain't seen the bridge!_____ (Spoken:) Where's that con-found - ed bridge?

Verse 3:
Oo, ain't gonna call me "Mister Pitiful," no, ah.
I don't need no respect from nobody, no, no.
Ah, ah, no, no, ah, ah.
I ain't gonna tell you nothin',
I ain't gonna tell ya no more, heck no!
She's my baby, let me tell you that I love her so and,
And she's the woman I really wanna love,
An' let me tell you more, oo!
She's my baby, let me tell ya she lives next door.
She's the one, a woman, the one, a woman that I know.
I ain't goin', I ain't gonna, I ain't gonna tell.
(To Outro:)

Chords used in this song:

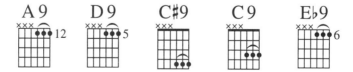

Dancing Days

Gtr. tuned in Open G:
⑥ = D ③ = G
⑤ = G ② = B
④ = D ① = D

Music and Lyrics by
Jimmy Page and Robert Plant

148

Dancing Days - 3 - 2
FBM0007

Verse 3:
You told your mama I'd get you home
But you didn't say that I got no car.
I saw a lion, he was standin' alone
With tadpole in a jar.

Chorus 3:
You know it's alright, I said, it's alright,
I guess it's all in my heart, heart, heart.
You'll be my only, my one and only.
Is that the way it should start?

Verse 4:
Said, dancin' days are here again
As the summer evenings grow.
You are my flower, you are my power,
You are my woman who knows.

Chorus 4:
I said, it's alright, y'know it's alright,
You know it's all in my heart.
You'll be my only, yes, my one and only, yes.
Is that the way it should start?
I know it isn't.

Chords used in this song:

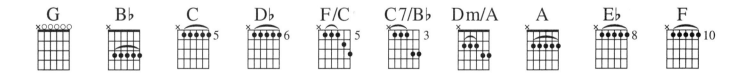

D'yer Mak'er

Music and Lyrics by
Jimmy Page, Robert Plant,
John Paul Jones and John Bonham

Oh, oh, oh, oh, oh,___ oh.___ Yeah!____ Ah, ah, ah, ah, ah, ah.___

Background vocal: (Why?)

REPEAT AD LIB. AND FADE

___ Oh._____ Ah, ah, ah,___ ah, ah._____

(Why?)

Verse 2:
Ay, ay, ay, ay, ay, ay,
All those tears I cry-ay, ay, ay, ay, ay,
All those tears I cry-ay, oh, oh, ay, ay,
Baby, please don't go.
(To Chorus:)

Verse 3:
Oh, oh, oh, oh, oh, oh,
Every breath I take, oh, oh, oh, oh, oh,
Every move I make, ay, ay, oh,
Baby, please don't go.

Verse 4:
Ay, ay, ay, ay, ay, ay,
You hurt me to my soul, oh, oh, oh, oh, oh,
You hurt me to my soul, oh, oh, oh, oh, oh,
Darling, please don't go.

Chorus 2:
When I read the letter that you sent me,
It made me mad, mad, mad.
When I read the news that it brought me,
You made me sad, sad, sad.
But I still love you so.
And I can't let you go.
I love you.
Ooh, a-baby, I love you.
(To Guitar solo)

Verse 5:
Oh, oh, oh, oh, oh, oh,
You don't have to go, oh, oh, oh, oh,
You don't have to go, oh, oh, oh, oh,
Oh, baby.
Babe! Please, please, please, please!
(To Coda)

Chords used in this song:

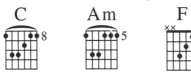

C   Am   F   G

No Quarter

Music and Lyrics by
Jimmy Page, Robert Plant
and John Paul Jones

Slowly (♩ = 66)
C#m7
Elec. Piano
(with pedal)

§ A Verse:
C#m7

1. *Elec. Piano plays melody as instrumental*
2. Close the door, put out the light.
3. *See additional lyrics*

You know they won't be home to-night.

C#m11   C#m7

Hm, hm, hm. The snow falls hard and don't you know

C#m11

the winds of Thor are blow-ing cold.

C#m7   B   A(#4)

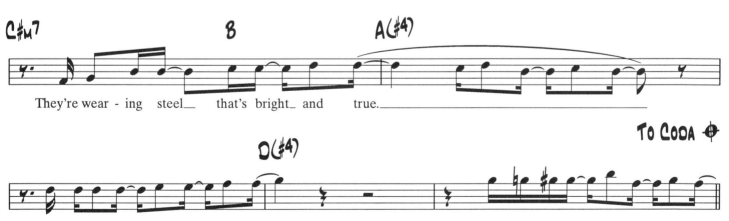

They're wear-ing steel that's bright and true.

To Coda ⊕

D(#4)

They car-ry news that must get through.

They choose the path where no one goes.

Verse 3:
Walking side by side with death,
The devil mocks their ev'ry step, Oo,
The snow drives back the foot that's slow.
The dogs of doom are howling more.
Oh, they carry news that must get through,
To build a dream for me and you.
They choose the path where no one goes.
(To Coda, Chorus:)

Chords used in this song:

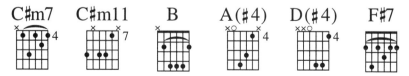

C#m7   C#m11   B   A(#4)   D(#4)   F#7

THE OCEAN

Music and Lyrics by
Jimmy Page, Robert Plant,
John Paul Jones and John Bonham

The Ocean - 3 - 1
FBM0007

157

2X: GUITAR SOLO AD LIB.

TO CODA ⊕ 1. 2.

D   C   Asus G+4 Asus C D   1.2.3.

4. Asus C D   F#5 G5   BRIDGE: A5   N.C.

La, la, la, la, la, la, la,____ la, la, la, la, la, la, la, la.

La, la, la, la, la, la, la,____ la, la, la, la, la, la, la, la.   La, la, la, la, la, la, la,____

____ la, la, la, la, la, la, la, la.   La, la, la, la, la, la, la,____ la, la, la, la, la, la, la, la.

D.S. 𝄋 AL CODA

⊕ CODA   SHUFFLE FEEL (♩ = 120)   D

The Ocean - 3 - 2
FBM0007

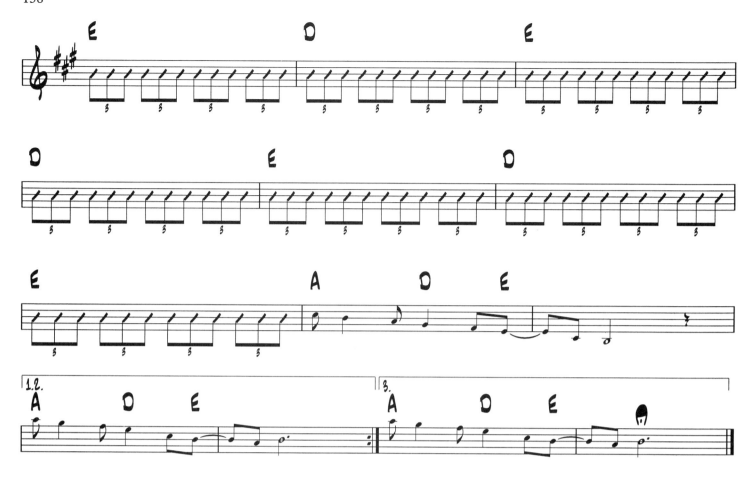

Verse 2:
Singin' to an ocean, I can hear the ocean's roar.
Play for free, I play for me, I play a whole lot more, more.
Singin' 'bout the good things and the sun that lights the day.
I used to sing to the mountains, has the ocean lost its way?

Verse 3:
Sitting 'round singing songs 'til the night turns into day.
Used to sing to the mountains but the mountains washed away.
Now I'm singing all my songs to the girl who won my heart.
She is only three years old and it's a real fine way to start.

Chords used in this song:

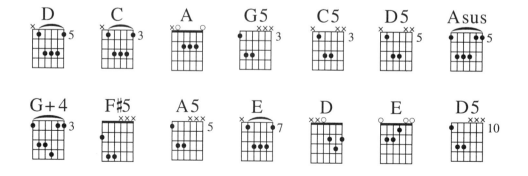

Custard Pie

Music and Lyrics by
Jimmy Page and Robert Plant

Moderately (♩ = 92)

A7

A Verse:
Riff cont.

1. Drop down, ba - by, yes,___ glad to see___ you. Drop down my way,___
2.-5. *See additional lyrics*

D

just dream of me. Well,___ my ma - ma al - low___ me,

C#5 C5   B5 B♭5   A7

I fool 'round all night long.

E5   G7sus

Well, I may look like I'm cra - zy,___

F5   G5   A7

I should know right___ from wrong.___

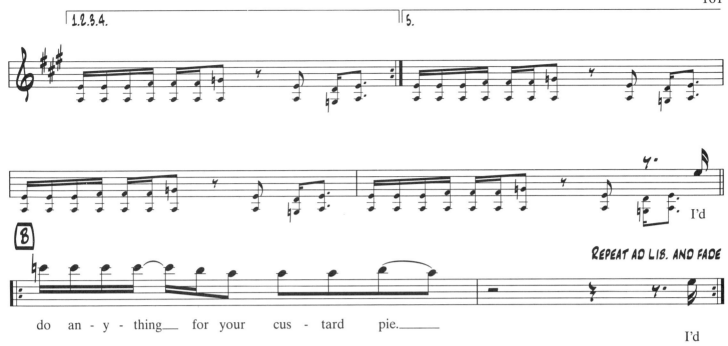

do an-y-thing___ for your cus-tard pie.___

I'd

I'd

REPEAT AD LIB. AND FADE

Verse 2:
See me comin', throw your man out the door.
Ain't no stranger, I've been this way before.
See me comin', throw your man out the door.
Ain't no stranger, I've been this way before.

Verse 3:
Put on your night shirt and your morning gown.
You know by now, I'm gonna shake 'em on down.
Put on your night shirt, mama and your morning gown.
You know by now, I'm sure gonna shake 'em on down.

Verse 4:
Guitar solo ad lib.

Verse 5:
Your custard pie, yeah, see it at night.
When you cut it, mama, save me a slice.
Your custard pic, I swear, I'll treat her nice.
(I like your custard pie.)
When you cut it, mama, please save me a slice.

Chords used in this song:

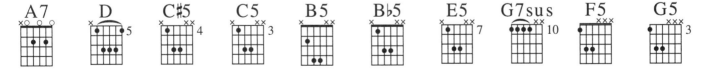

A7   D   C#5   C5   B5   Bb5   E5   G7sus   F5   G5

THE ROVER

Music and Lyrics by
Jimmy Page and Robert Plant

1. I've been to Lon - don,___ seen sev - en won - ders, I know to trip is just to
2.3. *See additional lyrics*

fall.   I used to rock___ it,   I used to roll___ it,___

I al - ways knew what it was_____ for._____

The Rover - 3 - 2
FBM0007

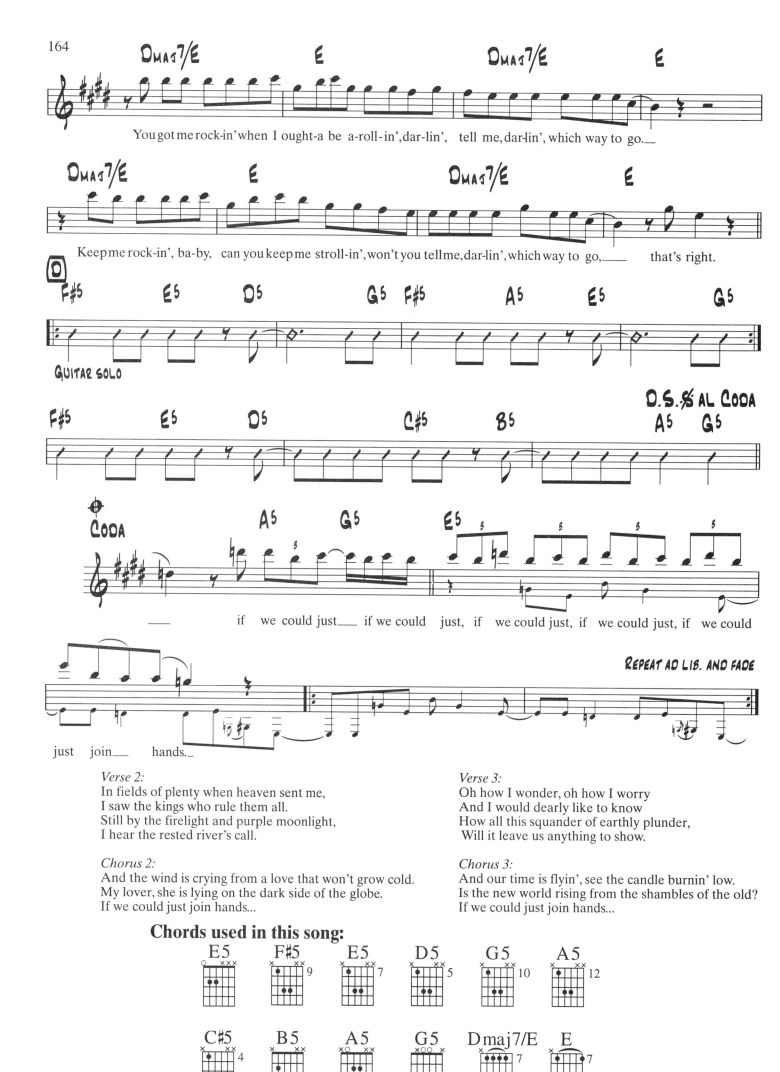

You got me rock-in' when I ought-a be a-roll-in', dar-lin', tell me, dar-lin', which way to go.

Keep me rock-in', ba-by, can you keep me stroll-in', won't you tell me, dar-lin', which way to go,_____ that's right.

GUITAR SOLO

D.S. % AL CODA

CODA

if we could just_____ if we could just, if we could just, if we could just, if we could

REPEAT AD LIB. AND FADE

just join_____ hands._

Verse 2:
In fields of plenty when heaven sent me,
I saw the kings who rule them all.
Still by the firelight and purple moonlight,
I hear the rested river's call.

Chorus 2:
And the wind is crying from a love that won't grow cold.
My lover, she is lying on the dark side of the globe.
If we could just join hands...

Verse 3:
Oh how I wonder, oh how I worry
And I would dearly like to know
How all this squander of earthly plunder,
Will it leave us anything to show.

Chorus 3:
And our time is flyin', see the candle burnin' low.
Is the new world rising from the shambles of the old?
If we could just join hands...

Chords used in this song:

E5   F#5   E5   D5   G5   A5

C#5   B5   A5   G5   Dmaj7/E   E

The Rover - 3 - 3
FBM0007

In My Time of Dying

Gtr. tuned in Open A:
⑥ = E ③ = A
⑤ = A ② = C#
④ = E ① = E

Words and Music by
Jimmy Page, Robert Plant,
John Paul Jones and John Bonham

1. In my time____ of dy - ing, want no - bod - y to moan.__
2. See additional lyrics

* Implied chords.

Verse 2:
Meet me, Jesus, meet me,
Oh, meet me in the middle of the air.
If my wings should fail me, Lord,
Oh please meet me with another pair.
(To Chorus:)

Bridge 2:
Oh! I did somebody good,
Somebody some good, yes?
Oh! I did somebody some good, yeah,
I must have done somebody some good, yeah.
(I believe I did.)
I see your smiling face, yeah,
And I know I must be meant to trace it.

Chords used in this song:

C5 B5 A5 D5 A D7 D13(#11) C7 C13(#11)

In My Time of Dying - 5 - 5
FBM0007

HOUSES OF THE HOLY

Music and Lyrics by
Jimmy Page and Robert Plant

Moderately fast (♩ = 120)

1. Let me take__ you to__ the mov - ies. Can I take__ you to__ the show?__
2.3. *See additional lyrics*

Let me be__ yours, ev - er tru - ly. Can I make__ your gar - den grow.__

(GTR. FILL)

From the hous - es of__ the ho - ly, we can watch__ the white_ doves go.__

TO CODA

From the door,__ comes Sa - tan's daugh - ter, and it on - ly goes__ to show,

Houses of the Holy - 2 - 1
FBM0007

and you know.____

(GTR. FILL)

Verse 2:
There's an angel on my shoulder,
In my hand, a sword of gold.
Let me wander in your garden.
And the seeds of love I'll sow, you know.
So the world is spinning faster.
Are you dizzy when you're stoned?
Let the music be your master.
Will you heed the master's call?

Verse 3:
Said, there ain't no use in crying.
'Cause it will only, only drive you mad.
Does it hurt to hear them lying?
Was this the only world you had?
So, let me take you, take you to the movies.
Can I take you, baby, to the show.
Why don't you let me be yours ever truly.
Can I make your garden grow?
And you know.

Chords used in this song:

A	A6	D	G	E

Trampled Underfoot

Words and Music by
Jimmy Page, Robert Plant
and John Paul Jones

Trampled Underfoot - 3 - 1
FBM0007

I can't stop talk - in'___ a-bout love.   I can't stop talk - in'___ a-bout

love.

Verse 2:
Trouble-free transmission helps your oil to flow.
Mama, let me pump your gas, mama, let me do it all.
Talkin' 'bout love...

Verse 3:
Check that heavy metal underneath your hood.
Baby, I could work all night, believe I've got the perfect tools
Talkin' 'bout love...

Verse 4:
A model built for comfort, really built with style.
Specialist tradition, mama, let me feast my eyes.
Talkin' 'bout love...

Verse 5:
Factory air-conditioned, heat begins to rise.
Guaranteed to run for hours, mama it's a perfect size.
Talkin' 'bout love...

Verse 6:
Groovin' on the freeway, gauge is on the red.
Gun down on my gasoline, I believe I'm gonna crack your head.
Talkin' 'bout love...

Verse 8:
Fully automatic, comes in any size.
Makes me wonder what I did, before we synchronized
Talkin' 'bout love...

Verse 9:
Feather-light suspension, coils just couldn't hold.
I'm so glad I took a look inside your showroom doors.
Talkin' 'bout love...

Chords used in this song:

Gm	Bb7	C7	Eb7	F7	G5

Kashmir

Kashmir - 3 - 1
FBM0007

176

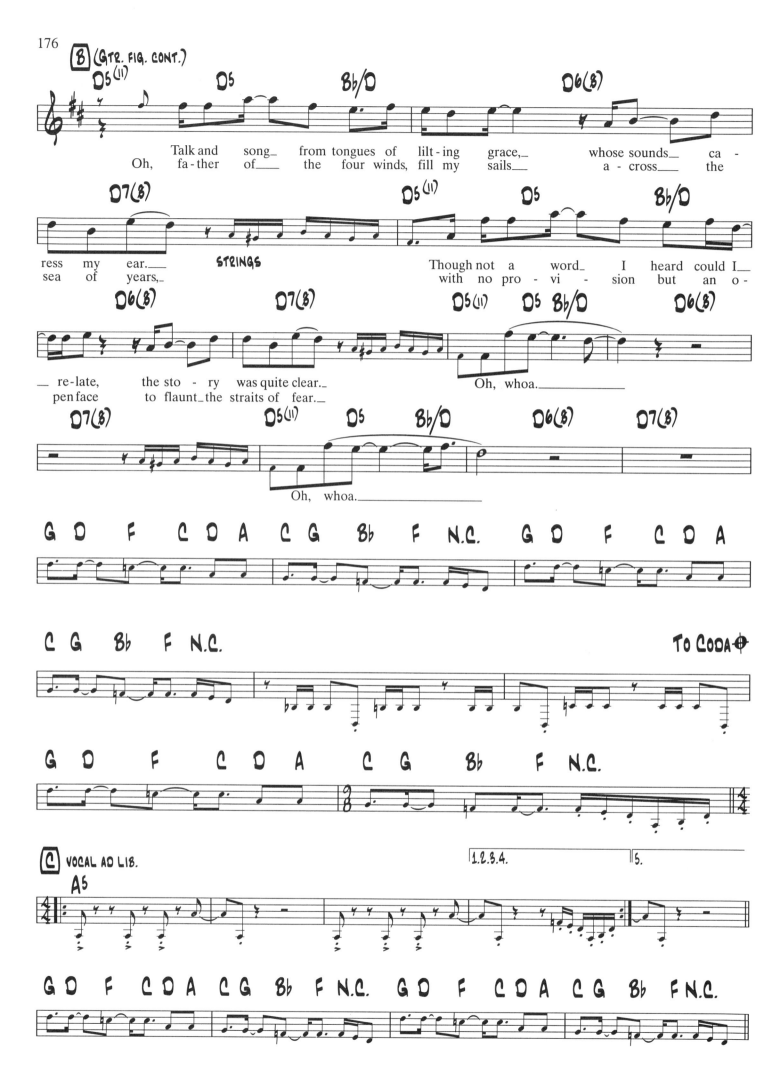

177

Chords used in this song:

Kashmir - 3 - 3
FBM0007

In the Light

Words and Music by
Jimmy Page, Robert Plant
and John Paul Jones

180

In the Light - 4 - 3
FBM0007

Verse 2:
Oh, baby, I just wanna show you,
What a clear view there is from every bend in the road.
Now listen, oh whoa, as I was relieved it will be for you too, honey
As you would for me. Oh, I will share your love.

Verse 3:
Hey! Oh, oh the winds of change may blow around you,
But that will always be so.
Oh, whoa, whoa, when love is pain it can devour you,
But you are never alone. I will share your love.

Chords used in this song:

In the Light - 4 - 4
FBM0007

Gtr. tuned to:
⑥ = C   ③ = G
⑤ = A   ② = C
④ = C   ① = E

BRON-YR-AUR

MUSIC BY
JIMMY PAGE

FAST (♩ = 172)

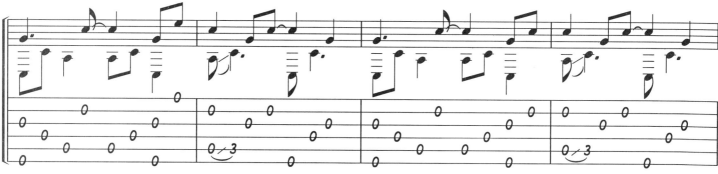

Bron-Yr-Aur - 4 - 2
FBM0007

DOWN BY THE SEASIDE

MUSIC AND LYRICS BY
JIMMY PAGE AND ROBERT PLANT

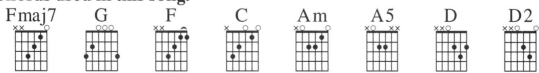

Verse 2:
Down in the city streets, see all the folk go racin', racin'.
No time left to pass the time of day.
The people turned away,
The people turned away, so far away, so far away.
See how they run, see how they run, etc.

Verse 3:
Out in the country, hear the people singin',
Singin' 'bout their progress, knowin' where they're goin'.
The people turned away,
The people turned away.

Verse 4:
Sing loud for the sunshine, pray hard for the rain,
And show your love for Lady Nature,
And she will come back again.
The people turned away,
The people turned away.
(To Coda)

Chords used in this song:

Fmaj7   G   F   C   Am   A5   D   D2

TEN YEARS GONE

Gtrs. in Drop D tuning:
⑥ = D ③ = G
⑤ = A ② = B
④ = D ① = E

Music and Lyrics by
Jimmy Page and Robert Plant

1. Then as it was, then a-gain it will be. Though the course may
2. Chang-es fill my time, babe, that's al-right with me. In the midst I

change some-time, riv-ers al-ways reach the sea.
think of you and how it use to be.

* BASS FUNCTION.

Ten Years Gone - 4 - 2
FBM0007

190

Ten Years Gone - 4 - 3
FBM0007

191

Chords used in this song:

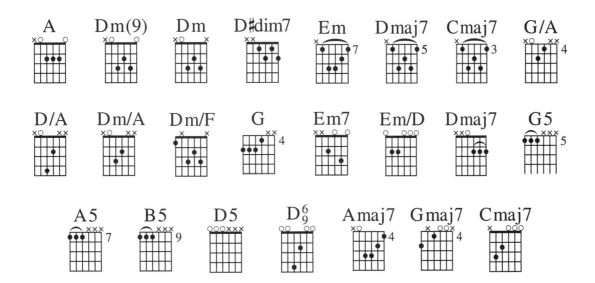

Night Flight

© 1975 Flames of Albion Music, Inc.
Copyright Renewed
All Rights for Flames of Albion Music, Inc. Administered by WB MUSIC CORP.
All Rights Reserved

194

Verse 2:
I just jumped a train that never stops.
So now, somehow, I know I'll never finish payin' for my ride.
Someone pushed a gun into my hand.
Tell me I'm the type of man to fight the fight without enquiring.
(To Chorus:)

Verse 3:
I once saw a picture of a lady with a baby.
Something made her have a very, very special smile.
We are in the middle of a change in destination.
When the train stops altogether, we will smile.
(To Chorus:)

Chords used in this song:

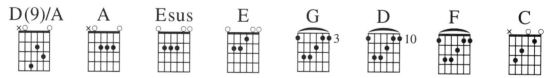

THE WANTON SONG

MUSIC AND LYRICS BY
JIMMY PAGE AND ROBERT PLANT

MODERATELY (♩ = 112)

Gtr. & Bass riff

A VERSE:
RIFF CONT.

1. Si - lent wom - an, in__ the night__ you came,__ took my seed from
2.3. *See additional lyrics*

my shak - ing frame. Same old fire,__ an - oth - er flame,

and the wheel rolls on.

Si - lent wom - an, through the flames__ you come,__ from the deep be - hind__ the

The Wanton Song - 3 - 1

FBM0007

196

The Wanton Song - 3 - 2
FBM0007

Verse 2:
Blazing eyes see the tremblin' hand.
Well, we know the time has come.
Lose my senses, lose command,
Feeling your healing rivers run.
Is it every time I fall, that I think this is the one?
In the darkness, can you hear me call?
Another day has just begun.

Verse 3:
Silent woman, how your face is changed.
Suddenly all the waves be calm.
Feel my fire needs a brand new flame
And the wheel rolls on, rolls on, rolls on, etc.

Chords used in this song:

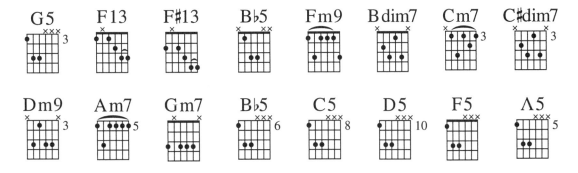

Boogie With Stu

Words and Music by
Jimmy Page, Robert Plant,
John Paul Jones, John Bonham,
Ian Stewart and Richie Valens

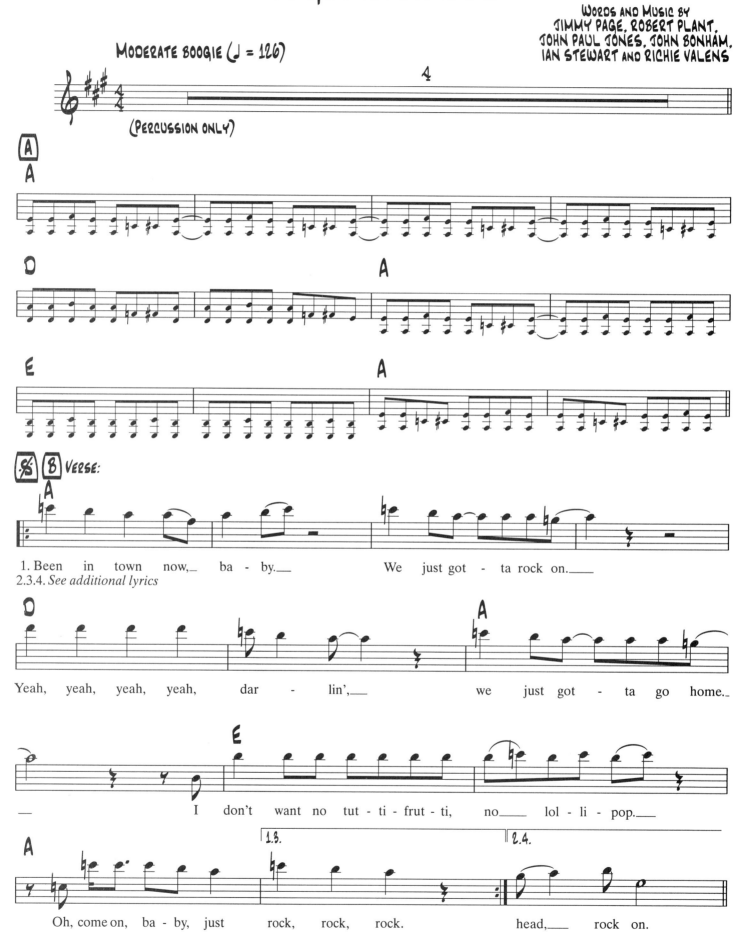

1. Been in town now,___ ba - by.___ We just got - ta rock on.___
2.3.4. *See additional lyrics*

Yeah, yeah, yeah, yeah, dar - lin',___ we just got - ta go home.___

___ I don't want no tut - ti - frut - ti, no___ lol - li - pop.___

Oh, come on, ba - by, just rock, rock, rock. head,___ rock on.

Ooh, ooh,___ ooh, ooh.___

Ooh, ooh,___ ooh, ooh.___   Ooh, ooh,___ ooh, ooh.___

I don't want no tut-ti-frut-ti, no___ lol-li-pop,___

Oh, come on, ba-by, just rock,___ rock,___ yeah.___   (PERCUSSION AND OUT)

Verse 2:
Yeah, yeah, yeah, yeah, honey,
We can shake it all night.
Whoa, whoa, whoa, whoa, darlin',
We just gotta roll right.
Ah, ooh, my head.
Rock on.

Verse 3:
Hey, babe, hey, babe. (4x)
I don't want no tutti-frutti, no lollipop.
Now, come on, baby, just rock, rock, rock.

Verse 4:
Ooh, ooh...etc.
Let's go!

Chords used in this song:

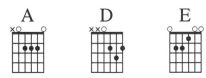

A   D   E

Black Country Woman

Gtr. tuned in Open G:
⑥ = D   ③ = G
⑤ = G   ② = B
④ = D   ① = D

Music and Lyrics by
Jimmy Page and Robert Plant

Moderately fast country blues (♩ = 122)

G7

INST. RIFF

1. Hey,_

A Verse:

RIFF CONT.

_ hey, ma - ma, what's the mat - ter here?_
2.3.4. *See additional lyrics*

Hey,___ hey, ma - ma, what's the mat - ter here?_

C7

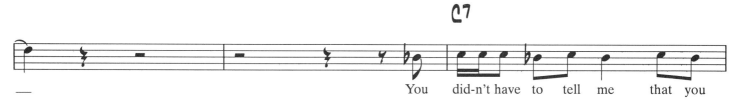

_ You did-n't have to tell me that you

Black Country Woman - 3 - 1
FBM0007

love me so.___ You did-n't have to tell me, ma - ma, let me go.___ Hey,_

G7

_ hey, ma - ma, what's the mat - ter here?___

C7

You did-n't have to make me a to - tal dis - grace.__

Did - n't have___ to leave me___ with that beer on my face.___ Hey,___

G7

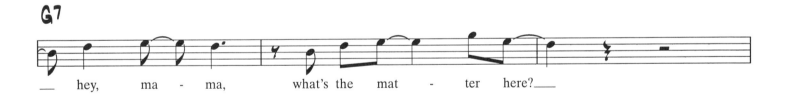

_ hey, ma - ma, what's the mat - ter here?___

D7   C7

But that's al - right,___ it's aw - ful dog-gone clear.

1.2.3.   4.

G7

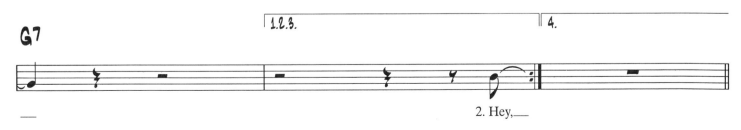

_   2. Hey,___

Black Country Woman - 3 - 2
FBM0007

202

Oh yeah yeah, oh yeah,___ oh yeah yeah.

Oh yeah yeah, oh yeah,___

oh.___

(Spoken:) What's the matter with you, mama?

Verse 2:
Hey, hey, baby, why you treat me mean?
Hey, hey, baby, why you treat me mean?
You didn't have to crucify me like you did.
You didn't have to tell me I was just your kid.
Hey, hey, mama, why'd you treat me mean?
You didn't have say you'd always be by my side.
You didn't have to tell me you'd be my blushin' bride.
Hey, hey, mama, why you treat me mean?
But that's alright, I know your sisters, too.

Verse 3:
(Inst. solo)
You didn't have to tell me that you love me so.
You didn't have to leave me, mama, let me go.
Hey, hey, mama, what is wrong with you?
You didn't have to leave me like a total disgrace.
You didn't have to leave me with that beer on my face.
Hey, hey, mama, what is wrong with you?
But that's alright, I'd be the same way, too.

Verse 4:
(Inst. solo)
You didn't have to crucify me like you did.
You didn't have to tell me I was just your kid.
Hey, hey, mama, what's the matter here?
You didn't have to tell me you would be my own.
You didn't have to tell me, baby, let me go.
Hey, hey, mama, what is wrong with you?
That's alright, I know your sister, too.

Chords used in this song:

Black Country Woman - 3 - 3
FBM0007

Sick Again

Music and Lyrics by
Jimmy Page and Robert Plant

1. From the win-dow of a
2.3.4. *See additional lyrics*

rent-ed lim-ou-sine,___ I caught your pret-ty blue eyes.___

One day soon, you're gon-na reach six - teen,___ *paint-ed la - dy in the cit-y of lies.*

Oh,___ Do you know my

name?_ Do I look the same?___

Sick Again - 3 - 2
FBM0007

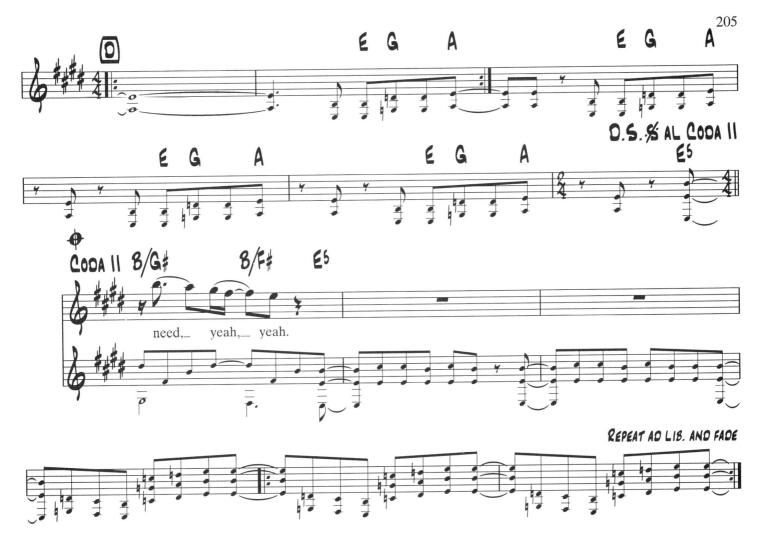

Verse 2:
Clutching pages from your teenage dream,
In the lobby of the Hotel Paradise.
Through the circus of the L.A. queens,
How fast you learn the downhill slide.
Oh, how you play the game.
Still don't know your name.
You know I'm the one you want, babe.
Yes, I got to be the one you need, need, need.
Yeah, yeah, yeah, yeah.

Verse 3:
Lips like cherries on the brown-eyed queen.
"Come on" flashed across your eyes.
Said you dug me since you were thirteen,
Then you giggle as you heave a sigh.
Oh, do you know my name?
Do I look the same?
Baby, I've got to tell you, I'm the one you want.
And everybody knows I'm the one you need.

Verse 4:
Hours, hours with a moment in between.
Oh, baby, how the time flies.
The fun of coming, all the pain in leaving.
Baby, dry those silver eyes.
Do you know my name?
Do I look the same?
You know I'm the one you want.
Ooh, ooh, yeah, yeah, 'cause I'm the one you need, yeah, yeah.

Chords used in this song:

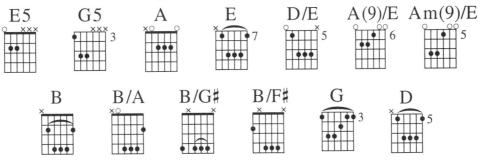

Sick Again - 3 - 3
FBM0007

ROYAL ORLEANS

MUSIC AND LYRICS BY
JIMMY PAGE, ROBERT PLANT,
JOHN PAUL JONES AND JOHN BONHAM

Royal Orleans - 3 - 2
FBM0007

Verse 2:
A man I know went down to Louisiana,
Had himself a bad, bad fright.
And when the sun peeks through,
Shone down on his Suzanna,
He kissed her whiskers left and right,
Whiskers.

Verse 3:
Now, a fight subsides
Out at a hotel in the quarter,
Our friendship took a bash tonight.
Now love gets hot, look far for a sea with water,
Grew whiskers sittin' there through the night.
(To Guitar solo)

Verse 5:
Now, a one time love,
Take care how you use it,
And try to make it last all night.
Take your pick,
Be careful how you choose it,
Sometimes it's hard to feel it bite.

Chords used in this song:

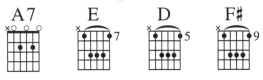

ACHILLES LAST STAND

Music and Lyrics by
Jimmy Page and Robert Plant

1. It was an A-pril morn-in' when they told us we___ should go,___
3. 5. *See additional lyrics*

and as I turned to you, you smiled at me, how could we say no?___

Achilles Last Stand - 6 - 1
FBM0007

214

Verse 3:
Into the sun, the south, the north,
At last the birds have flown,
The shackles of commitment fell,
In pieces on the ground.
Oh, to ride the wind,
To tread the air above the din,
Oh, to laugh aloud,
With dancing eyes we court the crowd, yeah.

Verse 4:
To seek the man whose pointing hand,
The giant step unfolds
To guide us from the curving path,
That churns up into stone.
If one bell should ring,
In celebration for a king,
So fast the heart should beat,
As proud's the head with heavy feet, yeah.

Verse 5:
The days went by when you and I,
Bathed in eternal summers glow,
As far away and distant,
Our mutual child did grow.
Whoa, the sweet refrain
Soothes the soul and calms the pain,
Oh, Albion remains,
Sleeping now to rise again.

Verse 6:
Wondering and wanderings,
One place to rest the search,
The mighty arms of Atlas,
Hold the heavens from the earth.
Oh, the mighty arms of Atlas,
Hold the heavens from the earth.
From the earth.
(To Outro:)

Chords used in this song:

FOR YOUR LIFE

Music and Lyrics by
Jimmy Page and Robert Plant

1. You said I was the on - ly,
   with my lem-on in your hand,__
2. 3. *See additional lyrics*

oh oh,____ oh oh.____

Ex - hi - bi-tion is your hab - it, e - mo - tion sec-ond hand,

oh oh,____ oh oh.____

For Your Life - 6 - 1
FBM0007

BRIDGE:

When you blow it, babe,_ you_____ got_ _ to blow it right.

Oh, ba - by, if you_ fake it, ma - ma,___ ba - by, fake with all your___ might._____

When you_ fake it,_____ ma - ma, please fake it right, *it's for your-self, babe.* When you f - f - f - fake_ it, ba - by,

you're fak-in' it for_ your life,_____ for your life,_____ for your life,_____ for your life.

Do it, do it, do it,___ do it, do it, do it when you wan - na.

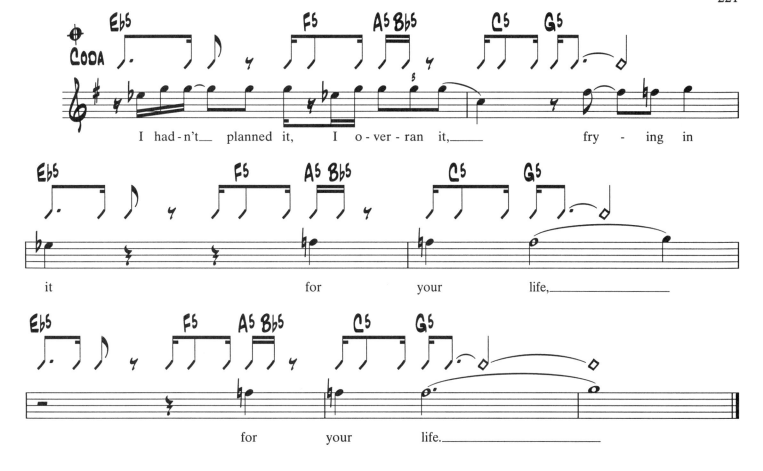

I had-n't___ planned it, I o-ver-ran it,_____ fry - ing in

it   for   your   life,_____

for   your   life._____

Verse 2:
Woo, woo, woo, woo.
Heard a cry for mercy,
In the city of the damned,
Oh oh, babe, deep down.
In the pits you go no lower,
The next stop's underground
Hello, underground.
Your wine and roses ain't quite over
Till favour deals a losing hand.
And I said:

Chorus 2:
Didn't mean to, did not convene to fluff it.
You didn't plan it, you over-ran it, ah.

Verse 3:
On the balance of a crystal, payin' through the nose,
(Snort!)
And when they couldn't resist you,
I thought you'd go with the flow.
And now your stage is empty,
Bring down the curtain, baby, please,
Fold up your show.

Chorus 3:
Hadn't planned to, could not stand to fry in it.
I hadn't planned it, I over-ran it, frying in it for your life,
For your life.

Chords used in this song:

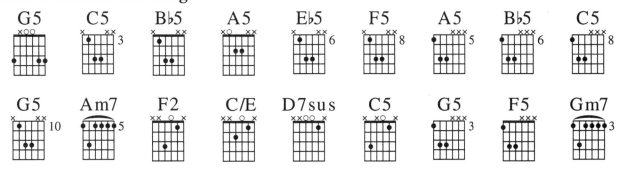

Candy Store Rock

Music and Lyrics by
Jimmy Page and Robert Plant

Candy Store Rock - 4 - 2
FBM0007

oh, ba-by, it's al-right, oh, it's al-right.

Oo,_____ oo,_____ it's al-right,_ it's

al-right. *REPEAT AD LIB. 5X* Oo,_____ oo,_____

yeah,_____ al-right._____

Verse 3:
Oh baby, baby, you're all that I wanted and more.
Oh baby, baby, I'm 'bout to kiss good-bye to the store.
Oh baby, baby, it ain't the wrapping that sells the goods.
Oh baby, baby, I got a sweet tooth but my mouth ain't full.
(To Chorus:)

Verse 4:
Oh baby, baby, oh you sting me like a bee.
Oh baby, baby, I like your honey and it sure likes me.
Oh baby, baby, I got my spoon inside your jar,
Oh baby, baby, don't give me too much, don't make me starve.

Verse 5:
Oh baby, baby, sugar sister on a silver plate,
Oh baby, baby, I need a mouthful and I just can't wait.
Oh baby, baby, see the shakin' in my hand,
Oh baby, baby, don't mean to fumble but it tastes so grand,
Tastes so grand...
(To Bridge:)

Chords used in this song:

F   A7   G5   A5   C5   D5   B5   G

Candy Store Rock - 4 - 4
FBM0007

Hots on for Nowhere

Music and Lyrics by
Jimmy Page and Robert Plant

Moderate sixteenth-note Shuffle (♩ = 96)

Bass & Rhythm

1. I was

A Verse:

E7 simile

burned in the heat of the mo - ment, though it could-'ve been the heat of the day,___ when I
2.3.4. *See additional lyrics*

learned how my time had been wast - ed___ a tear fell as I turned a-way. Now I've got

friends who will give me their shoul - der___ e - vent I should hap-pen to fall._____ With

time and his bride_ grow-ing old - er___ I got friends who will give me fuck all.___

B Chorus:

La la la la la la la la,___ yeah. La la la la la la la la___ la, ba - by. La

To Coda 🎯 1. 2.

A7

la la la la la la la la,___ yeah.. La la la la la la la la la.

Hots on for Nowhere - 4 - 1
FBM0007

228

Hots on for Nowhere - 4 - 3
FBM0007

Verse 2:
Corner of Bleeker and nowhere,
In the land of not quite day,
A shiver ran down my backbone,
Face in the mirror turns grey.
So looked around to hitch from a reindeer
Searchin' hard tryin' to brighten the day.
I turned around to look for the snowman,
To my surprise he'd melted away, yeah.
(To Chorus:)

Verse 3:
The moon and the stars out of order,
Inside my tides dance the ebb and sway,
The sun in my soul's sinking lower
While the hope in my hands turns to clay.
I don't ask that my field's full of clover,
I don't moan at opportunity's door.
Why don't you ask my advice, take it slower
Then your story'd be your finest reward.
(To Chorus:)

Verse 4:
Lost on the path to attainment,
Search in the eyes of the wise.
When I bled from the heart of the matter,
I started bleeding without a disguise.
Now everything's fine under heaven,
Now and then you gotta take time to pause.
And if you're down on the ground,
Don't be messin' around
Or you'll land in a boat without oars.
(To Chorus:)

Chords used in this song:

E7   A7   E   D   A   A5

Hots on for Nowhere - 4 - 4
FBM0007

Tea for One

Music and Lyrics by
Jimmy Page and Robert Plant

ba-by, when I feel____ this way.____

A min-ute seems like a life - time, oh ba - by, oh when I

feel this way,_ I feel this way.____

Bridge 2:
To sing a song for you,
I recall you used to say,
Oh baby, this one's for we two,
Which in the end is you anyway.
How come twenty-four hours, baby,
Sometimes seem to slip into days?
A minute seems like a lifetime,
Oh baby, when I feel this way.
(To Verse 2:)

Chords used in this song:

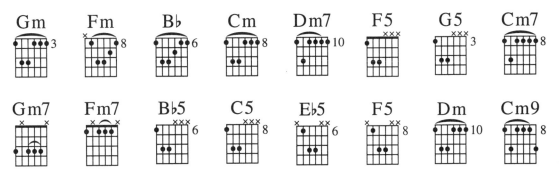

Nobody's Fault But Mine

Music and Lyrics by
Jimmy Page and Robert Plant

Nobody's Fault but Mine - 3 - 2
FBM0007

236

Verse 2:
Devil, he told me to roll.
Devil, he told me to roll.
How to roll but not collide.
Nobody's fault but mine.
(To Blues Harp solo)

Verse 3:
Brother, he showed me the gong,
Brother, he showed me the ding, dong, ding, dong.
How to kick that gong, delight,
Oh, it's nobody's fault but mine.

Verse 4:
Got a monkey on my back,
A m, m, m, m, monkey on my back, back, back, back,
Gonna change my ways tonight,
Nobody's fault but mine.
(To Guitar solo)

Chords used in this song:

E   A5   D   E   F#5   G5   A

Nobody's Fault but Mine - 3 - 3
FBM0007

In the Evening

MUSIC AND LYRICS BY
JIMMY PAGE, ROBERT PLANT
AND JOHN PAUL JONES

In the Evening - 4 - 1
FBM0007

Verse 3:
Ooh, it's simple,
All the pain that you go through.
You can't turn away from fortune, fortune, fortune,
'Cause that's all that's left to you.
Hey, it's lonely at the bottom,
Man, it's dizzy at the top.
But if you're standing in the middle, oh,
Ain't no way you're gonna stop.
(To Chorus:)

Verse 4:
Instrumental solo ad-lib.
(To Interlude:)

Verse 5:
Ooh, whatever
What your days may bring.
No use in hiding in a corner
'Cause that won't change a thing.
If you're dancing in the doldrums,
One day soon it's gotta stop.
When you're master of the off-chance,
Well, you don't expect a lot.
(To Coda)

Chords used in this song:

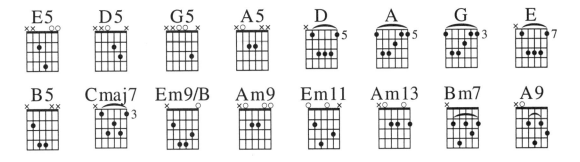

SOUTH BOUND SUAREZ

MUSIC AND LYRICS BY
JOHN PAUL JONES AND ROBERT PLANT

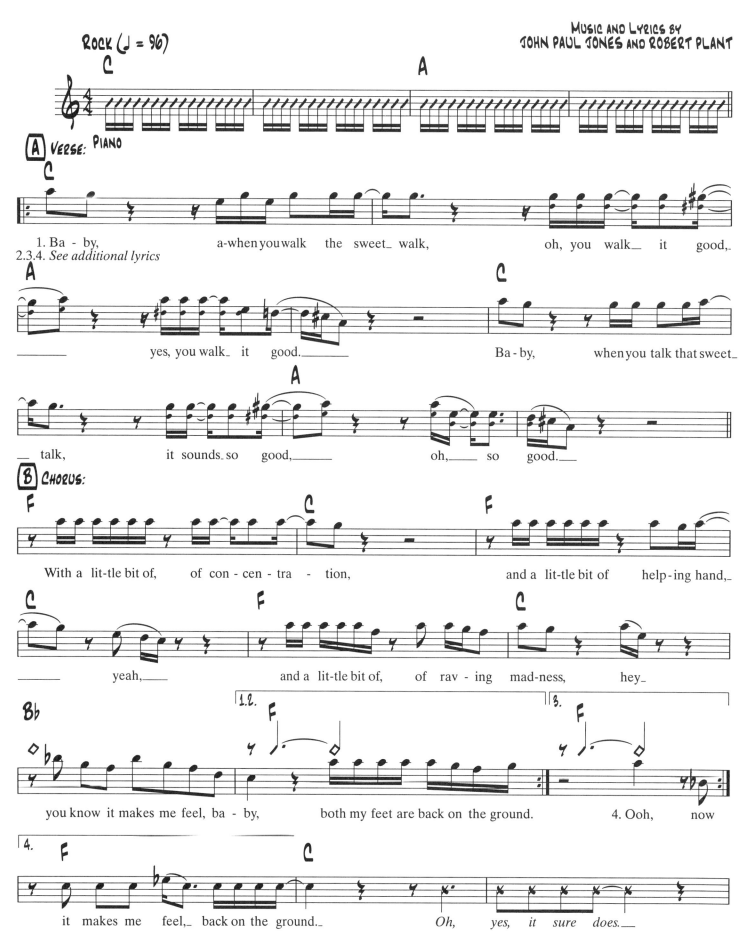

South Bound Suarez - 2 - 1
FBM0007

243

It makes me feel,___ hey,___ yeah, back on the ground.___ Suar-ez,___

Suar-ez,___ ba-by, ba-by. You're_____ back on___

the ground._____ I'm good, yeah, I'm feel-ing

good, yeah, hey, I'm feel-ing good, yeah. I'm feel-ing good, yeah, hey._

Back on the ground._ Sha-la-la-la, sha-la-la-la___ la-la-la.

REPEAT AD LIB. AND FADE

Sha-la-la-la, sha-la-la-la, la-la-la. Sha-la-la-la, sha-la-la-la,___ la-la-la.

Verse 2:
And when the rhythm takes me
It feels so good, oh so good.
Baby, if it keeps a-shaking
It will do you good, oh so much good.

Chorus 2:
With a little bit of stop-a-shakin' shakin'
And a little bit of fly right down,
And a little bit of sweet con-carne,
It makes me feel, makes me feel
I got my feet on the ground.

Verse & Chorus 3:
Instrumental solo ad lib.

Verse 4:
Ooh now, baby, when you move it makes me
Really feel so good, oh so good.
And I'm so glad, so glad, so glad, so glad
And I'm good, oh, so good.

Chorus 4:
With a little bit of concentration
And a little bit of helping hand,
And a little bit of raving madness,
It makes me feel, yeah,
Back on the ground.

Chords used in this song:

C A F Bb

South Bound Suarez - 2 - 2
FBM0007

FOOL IN THE RAIN

Music and Lyrics by
Jimmy Page, Robert Plant
and John Paul Jones

246

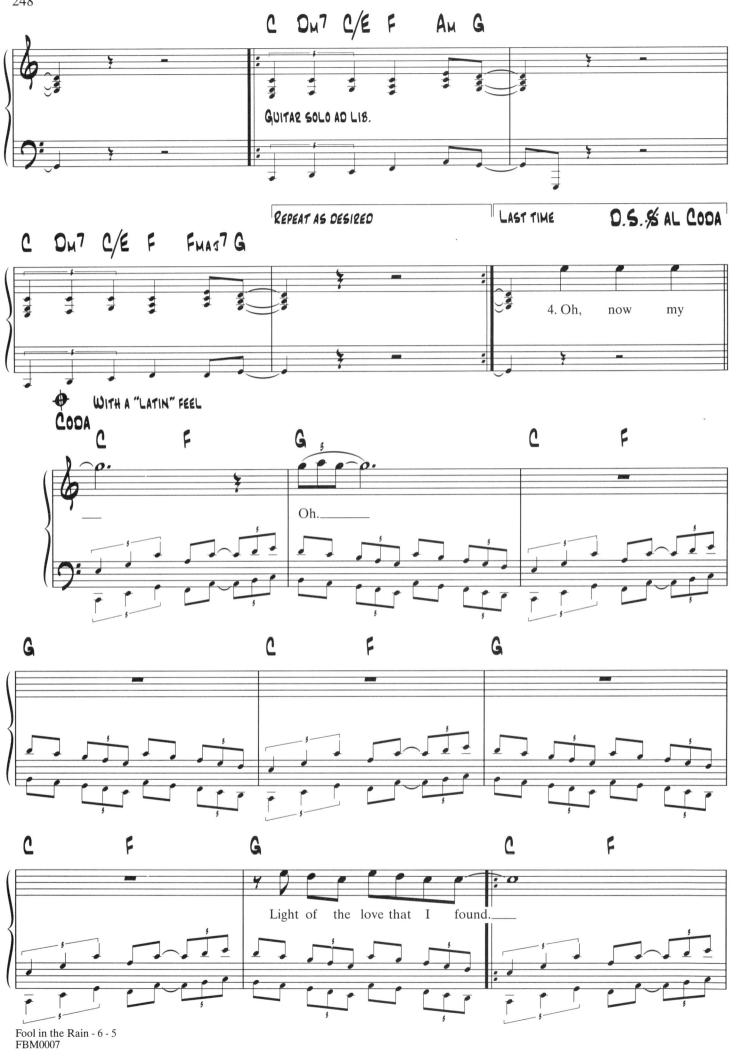

Chords used in this song:

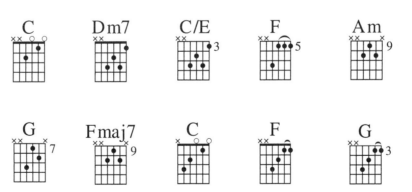

Hot Dog

Music and Lyrics by
Jimmy Page and Robert Plant

251

Hot Dog - 3 - 2
FBM0007

252

Chords used in this song:

Hot Dog - 3 - 3
FBM0007

CAROUSELAMBRA

Music and Lyrics by
John Paul Jones, Jimmy Page
and Robert Plant

1. Sis - ters of the way - side bide their time in qui - et peace,_ a -
2.3. *See additional lyrics*

wait their place with-in the ring of calm._ Still stand to turn in

sec - onds of re - lease,_ a - wait the call they know may nev - er come._

In times of light - ness, no in - trud - er dared up - on to

jeop - ar - dize the course, up - set the run._ All was joy and hands were raised_

254

255

1. Where was your word,___ where did you go?___
2. Dull is the ar-mour, cold is the day.___
3. I heard the word,___ I could-n't stay.___

Where was your help-ing, where was your bow,___
Hard was the jour-ney, hard was the way,___
I could-n't stand___ it an-oth-er day,___

Carouselambra - 5 - 3
FBM0007

Held now with in the know - ing, rest now with - in the peace,_

take of the fruit but guard___ the seed._____
Take of the fruit but guard___ the seed._____

A B7   A B7   A B7

REPEAT AD LIB. AND FADE

A B7 |1. |2. C   C A B7   C

Verse 2:
Still in their bliss unchallenged mighty feast,
Unending dances shadowed on the day.
Within the walls, their daunting formless keep,
Preserved their joy and kept their doubts at bay.
Faceless legions stood in readiness to weep.
Just turn a coin, bring order to the fray.
And everything is soon no sooner thought than deed,
But no one seemed to question anyway.
(To Chorus:)

Verse 3:
How keen the storied hunter's eye
Prevails upon the land
To seek the unsuspecting and the weak.
And powerless the fabled sat, too smug to lift a hand
Toward the foe that threatened from the deep.
Who cares to dry the cheeks of those who saddened stand
Adrift upon a sea of futile speech?
And to fall to fate and make the "status plan."
(To Chorus:)

Chords used in this song:

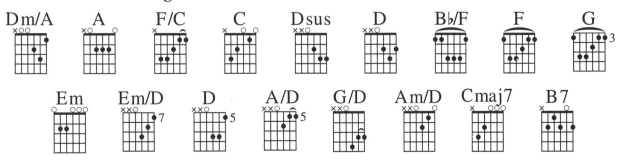

Dm/A A F/C C Dsus D Bb/F F G
Em Em/D D A/D G/D Am/D Cmaj7 B7

I'm Gonna Crawl

Music and Lyrics by
Jimmy Page, Robert Plant
and John Paul Jones

1. Oh,_____ she's my ba-by, let me tell you why.
2.3. *See additional lyrics*

Hey, she drives_ me cra-zy, she's the ap-ple of my eye._____

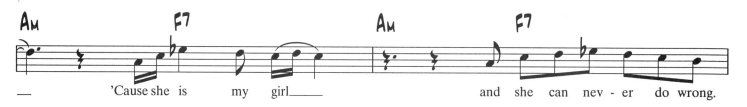

_ 'Cause she is my girl_____ and she can nev-er do wrong.

I'm Gonna Crawl - 2 - 1
FBM0007

See additional lyrics

PLAY 5X

Verse 2:
Hey, I love that little lady,
I got to be her fool.
Ain't no other like my baby,
I can break the golden rule.
'Cause I get down on my knees,
Oh, and I pray that love won't die.
And if I always try to please,
And don't know the reason why.

Verse 3:
Instrumental solo ad lib.

Coda
I don't have to go by plane, I ain't got to go by car.
I don't care where my darlin' is, people, I don't care how far.
I'm gonna crawl, I'm gonna crawl. I don't care if I got to go back home.
I don't care what I got to stand to get to you. I'm gonna crawl,
I'm gonna crawl, ah, I'm gonna move the car, baby.
I say, she give good lovin', she give me good lovin',
She give me good lovin', she give me good lovin',
My baby give me good lovin', oh, yes, I love her,
I guess I love her, yes, I love her, I wanna crawl.

Chords used in this song:

C	Ab	G+	Am	F7	D7	G7	C⁶/₉

All My Love

Music and Lyrics by
John Paul Jones and Robert Plant

A Verse 1:
1. Should I fall out of love, my fire in the light,___ to chase a feath-er in the wind.

With-in the glow_ that weaves a cloak of de-light,___ there moves a thread that has_ no end.

B Verses 2, 3, & 4:
2. For man-y hours___ and days that pass___ ev-er soon,___
3. The cup is raised,___ the toast is made_ yet a-gain,___
4. Yours is the cloth,___ mine is the hand_ that sews time,___

the tides have caused a flame_ to dim. At last the arm_ is straight, the
one voice is clear a-bove_ the din. Proud Ar-y-an,___ one word my
his is the voice that lies___ with-in. Ours is the fire,___ all the

hand to the loom,___ is this the end_ or just___ be-gin?___
will to sus-tain,___ for me the cloth once more___ to spin.___
warmth we can find,___ he is the feath-er in___ the wind.___

C Chorus:
All of my love,___ all of my love,___ oh all of my love___ to

262

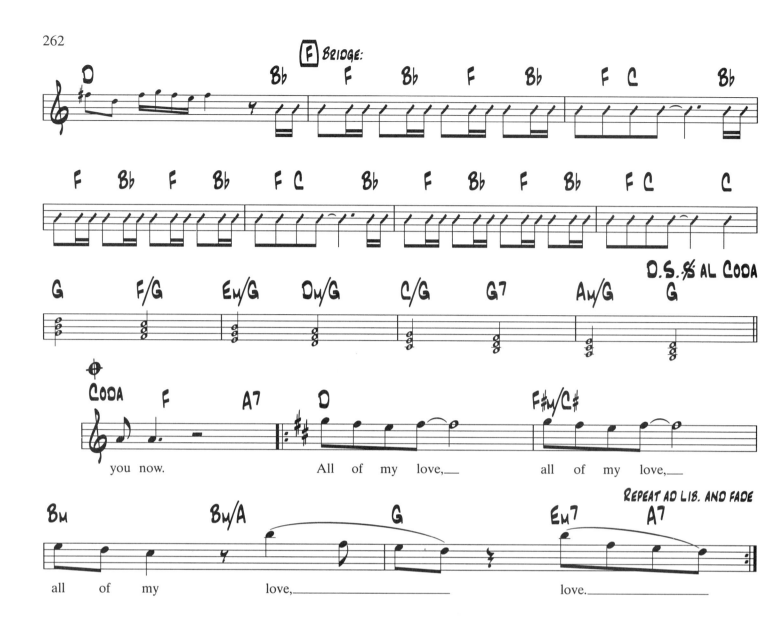

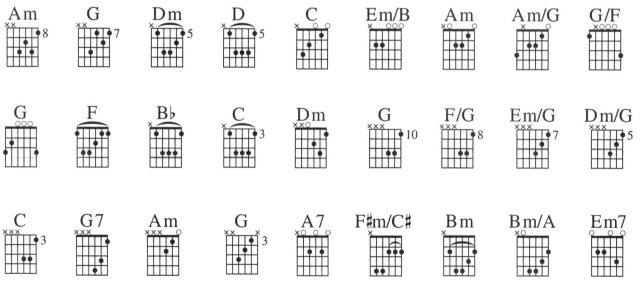

Chords used in this song;

Am G Dm D C Em/B Am Am/G G/F

G F Bb C Dm G F/G Em/G Dm/G

C G7 Am G A7 F#m/C# Bm Bm/A Em7

All My Love - 3 - 3
FBM0007

CODA

LED·ZEPPELIN

Poor Tom

Gtr. tuned in Open C:
⑥ = C   ③ = G
⑤ = G   ② = C
④ = C   ① = E

Music and Lyrics by
Jimmy Page and Robert Plant

Bright Delta Blues (♩ = 100)
Guitar tacet

drums

A Verse 1:

N.C.

1. Here's the tale___ of Tom___ who worked the rail - roads long.___

___ His wife would cook___ his meal,___ as

he would change___ the wheel.___ Sing poor Tom,___

sev - enth son,___ al - ways knew__ what's go - in' on.___

Am   E+/G#   C/G

Ain't no thing___ that you can hide___ from Tom.___

C   Am   E+/G#

And there ain't___ no thing__ that you can hide___ from Tom.___

266

you can hide___ from Tom.

3. His

What a - bout___ that grand - son on___ your knee?___

Rail - road songs,___ Tom would sing___ to me.___

There ain't____ no thing__ that you___ can hide__ from Tom.__

There ain't no thing___ that

Verse 3:
His wife was Annie May,
With any man, she'd play.
When Tom was out of town
She couldn't keep her dresses down.
Poor Tom, seventh son.
Always knew what's goin' on.
Ain't no thing that you can hide from Tom.

Verse 4:
So it was one day,
People got to Annie May.
Tom stood, a gun in his hand,
Stoppin' her runnin' 'round.
Poor Tom, seventh son.
You gotta die for what you done.
All those years of work done thrown away,
To ease your mind, is all that you can say.

Chords used in this song:

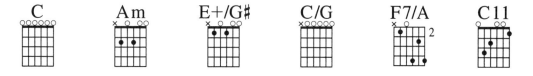

Walter's Walk

Music and Lyrics by
Jimmy Page and Robert Plant

CODA

E5

ter now?__

D5 E5

Does it mat - ter now?_____

REPEAT AD LIB. AND FADE

D5 E5

Verse 2:
Every tear that falls is a smile that's lost.
When you hear the call can you count the cost?
As you stand alone do you wonder how?
Can you step aside, does it matter now?

Every love that's changed, every love that's changed,
In the eye of the night, in the eye of the night,
In the day everything, in the day everything.
She was smilin' a tear as her waters fall.

You know it's true. You know it's true now.

Verse 3:
Instrumental solo ad lib.

I'm walkin' the floor over you.
I'm walkin' the floor.

Every tear that falls is a smile that's lost.
When you hear the call can you count the cost?
As you stand alone do you wonder how?
Can you step aside, does it matter now?

Chords used in this song:

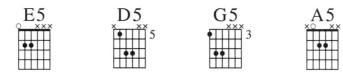

Jimmy Page, 1975
© Bob Alford/Star File

Ozone Baby

Music and Lyrics by
Jimmy Page and Robert Plant

1. I hear you knock on my door,___ I ain't been sav-in' this scene_
2. *See additional lyrics*

___ for ya, hon-ey. Don't want-cha ring-in' my bell,_

___ it's too late___ for you to be my hon-ey.

Oo,_____ it's my love.___ Oo,_____ it's my own

___ true love.___ Oo,_____ it's my love.___

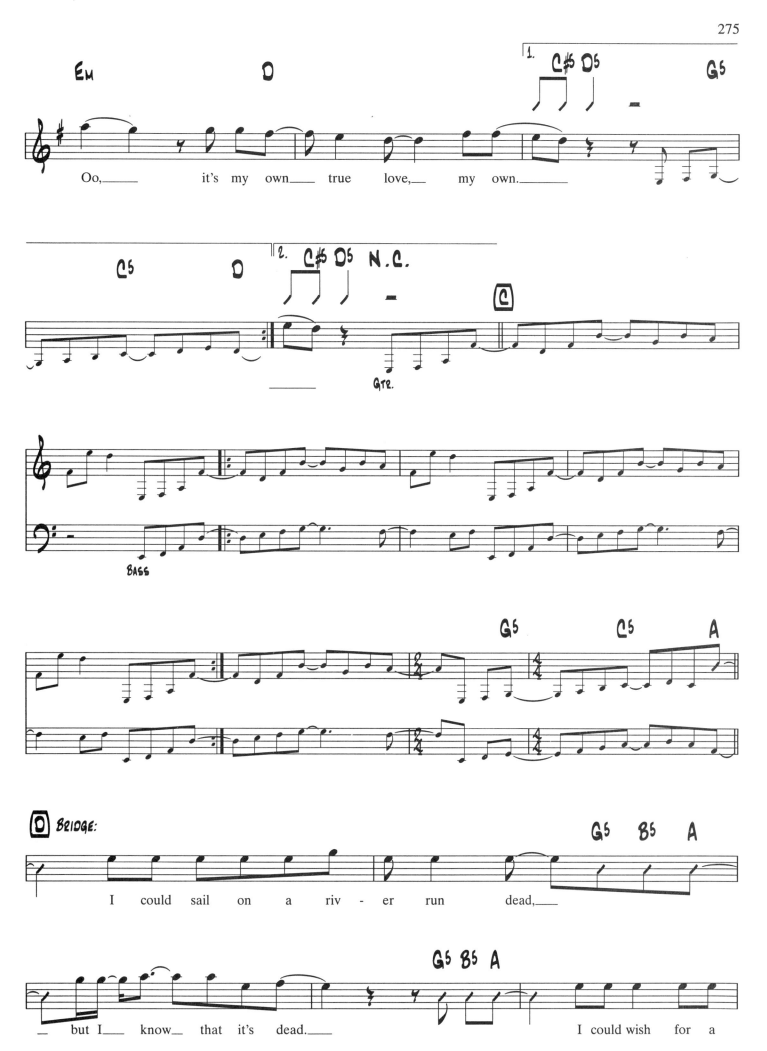

276

Verse 2:
Don't want you wasting my time,
Tired of ya doing the things that you do.
It's no use standing in line,
Follow the line, you better follow the queue.
(To Chorus:)

Chords used in this song:

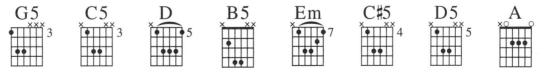

G5   C5   D   B5   Em   C#5   D5   A

Darlene

Music and Lyrics by
John Bonham, John Paul Jones,
Jimmy Page and Robert Plant

Darlene - 5 - 2
FBM0007

280

What you got is sure___ is fine,___

1.   2.

I wan - na get me some.___   Dar - sick.

C GUITAR SOLO: (♩♩ = ♩³♩)

G   G/F   C/E   G   G/F   C/E

G   G/F   C/E

G7   1.   2.   Bb B C

D PIANO SOLO:
Bb B C   Bb B C Bb B C   Bb B C   Bb B C Bb B C

Bb B C   Bb B C C#D N.C.   1.   Bb B C   2.   Bb5

C5   D5   1.   Bb5   2.

Darlene - 5 - 3
FBM0007

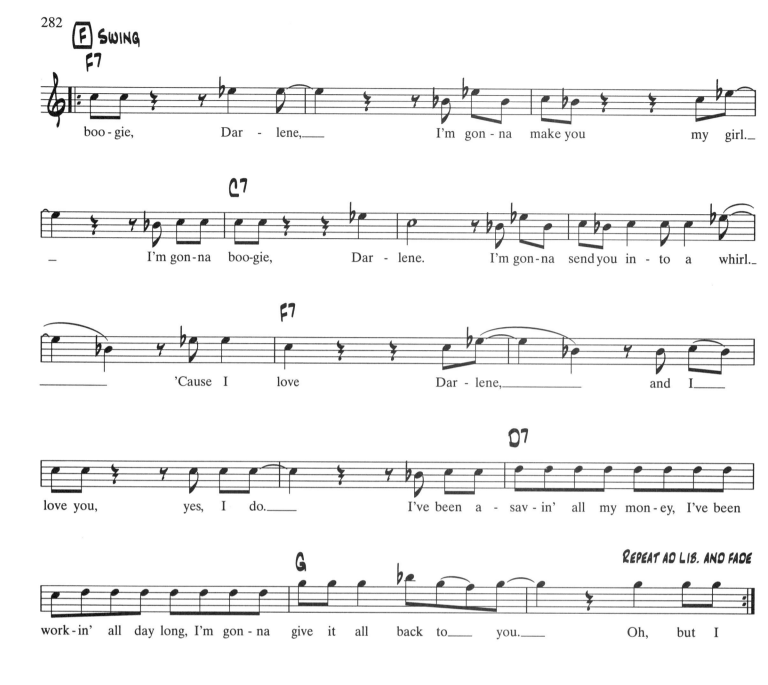

Verse 2:
When I see you on the street,
Makes my heart go flip.
I see you walkin' with all those guys
And make me feel so sick.
(To Guitar solo:)

Chords used in this song:

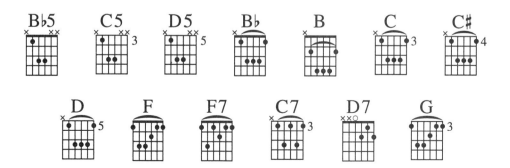

Led Zeppelin, 7/15/1973
© 2004 Bob Gruen/Star File

Wearing and Tearing

Music and Lyrics by
Jimmy Page and Robert Plant

Verse 2:
Oh, don't you feel the same way?
Oh, don't you feel the same way?
But you don't know what to do.
No time to hesitate,
Ain't no time for hesitatin',
All you got to do is groove.
They say you're feelin' blue, well,
I just found a cure,
It's a thing you gotta do, yeah.
(To Chorus:)

Verse 3:
Now listen:
You say your body's aching,
I know that it's aching,
Chill bumps come up on you.
Yeah, the funny fool,
I love the funny fool,
Just like foolin' after school.
And then you ask for medication,
Who cares about medication
When you've worn away the cure.
(To Chorus:)

Verse 4:
Go back to the country,
Yeah, go back to the country,
Feel a change is good for you.
When you keep convincin',
Ah, don't keep convincin',
But what's that creeping up behind you?
It's just an old friend,
It's just an old friend,
And what's that he's got for you?
(To Chorus:)

Chords used in this song:

HEY, HEY WHAT CAN I DO

Music and Lyrics by
Jimmy Page, Robert Plant,
John Paul Jones and John Bonham

1. I wan-na tell you 'bout the girl I love,_ my she looks so fine._
2.3. *See additional lyrics*

Ah, she's the on-ly one that I been dream-ing of,_ may-be some-day she will be all mine._

I wan-na tell her that I love her so,_ I thrill with her ev-'ry touch._

I need to tell her she's the on-ly one I real-ly love._

I've got a wom-an wan-na ball all day._

Hey, Hey What Can I Do - 2 - 1
FBM0007

I've___ got a wom - an, she won't be true___ now.___

I've got a wom - an, stay drunk___ all the time._____

1.2.

I said I got a lit - tle wom-an and she won't be true._____

3.

got a lit - tle wom-an and she won't be true.___

(Hey   hey,   what_ you gon-na do?)

Repeat ad lib. and fade

Whoa   whoa,   what_ you gon-na say?)

Verse 2:
On Sunday morning when we go down to church, see the men folk standing in line.
They say they've come to pray to the Lord, but when my little girl looks so fine.
And in the evening when the sun is sinking low, and everybody's with the one they love,
I walk the town, keep a-searchin' all around, lookin' for my street corner girl.
(To Chorus:)

Verse 3:
And in the bars where men play guitars and a-drinkin' and rememberin' the time,
My little lover does a midnight shift, she fool around all the time.
I guess there's just one thing left for me to do, gonna pack my bags and move away.
Because I got a worried mind, sharing what I thought was mine, gonna leave her where the guitars play.
(To Chorus:)

Chords used in this song:

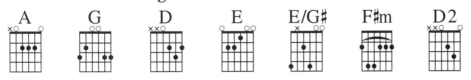

A   G   D   E   E/G#   F#m   D2

Selected Riffs

ACHILLES LAST STAND
(Guitar Riff)

Music and Lyrics by
Jimmy Page and Robert Plant

BABE, I'M GONNA LEAVE YOU
(Guitar Riff)

Music and Lyrics by
Anne Bredon, Jimmy Page, and Robert Plant

FBM0007

BRING IT ON HOME
(Guitar Riffs)

Willie Dixon and J.B. Lenoir

BLACK DOG
(Guitar Riff)

Words and Music by
Jimmy Page, Robert Plant
and John Paul Jones

All gtrs. tuned to Open G:
⑥ = D   ③ = G
⑤ = G   ② = B
④ = D   ① = D

DANCING DAYS
(Guitar Riff)

MUSIC AND LYRICS BY
JIMMY PAGE AND ROBERT PLANT

0:00

MODERATE ROCK (♩ = 116)
INTRO:
Gtrs. 3 & 4 (w/slide)

PLAY REPEATS SIMILE

Gtrs. 1 & 2

PLAY REPEATS SIMILE

0:17

1.

2.

TO VERSE:
Bb5 C5

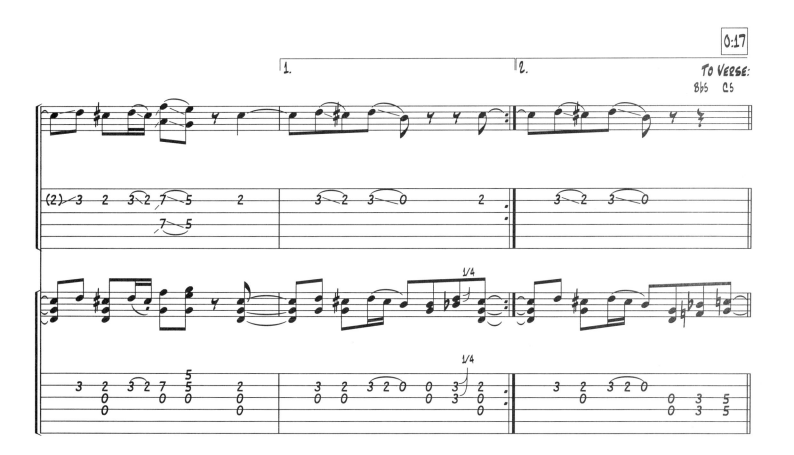

Dazed and Confused
(Interludes)

Music and Lyrics by
Jimmy Page

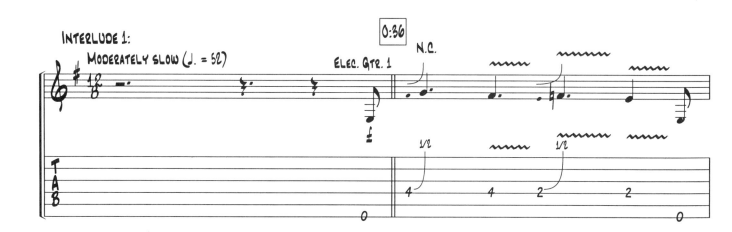

Good Times Bad Times
(Guitar Riff)

Music and Lyrics by
Jimmy Page, John Paul Jones
and John Bonham

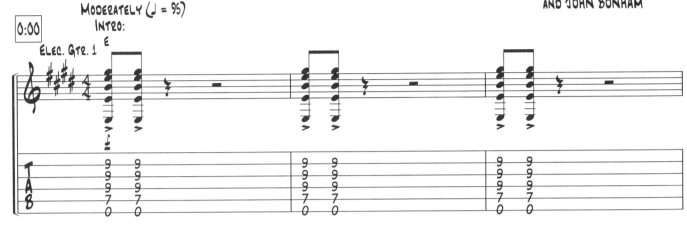

Two Gtrs. Arr. for One.

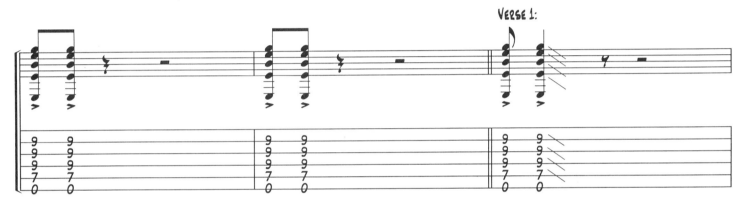

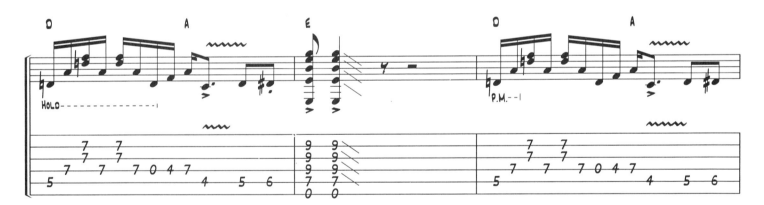

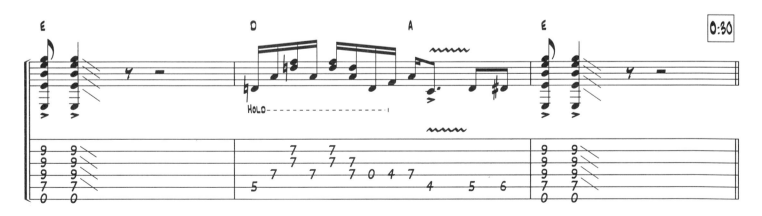

Heartbreaker
(Guitar Riff)

Music and Lyrics by
Jimmy Page, Robert Plant,
John Paul Jones and John Bonham

Houses of the Holy
(Guitar Riff)

Music and Lyrics by
Jimmy Page and Robert Plant

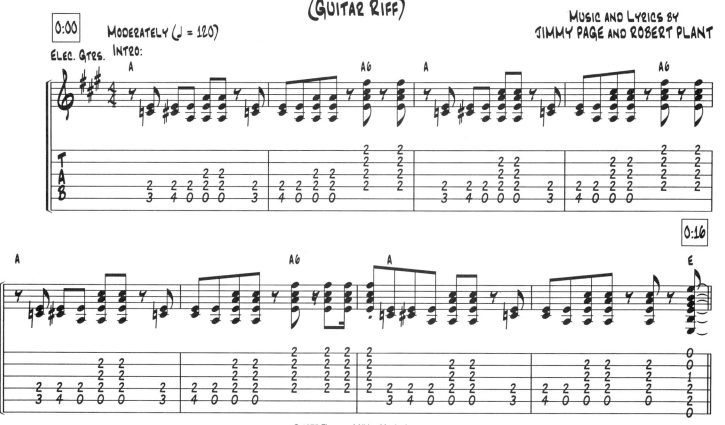

FBM0007

COMMUNICATION BREAKDOWN
(Intro Riff)

Music and Lyrics by
Jimmy Page, John Paul Jones
and John Bonham

HOW MANY MORE TIMES
(Guitar Riff)

Music and Lyrics by
Jimmy Page, John Paul Jones
and John Bonham

IMMIGRANT SONG
(Guitar Riff)

Music and Lyrics by
Jimmy Page and Robert Plant

M0007

Gtrs. tuned to DADGAD:
⑥ = D ③ = G
⑤ = A ②ة = A
④ = D ① = D

KASHMIR
(Guitar Riffs)

Words and Music by
Jimmy Page, Robert Plant
and John Bonham

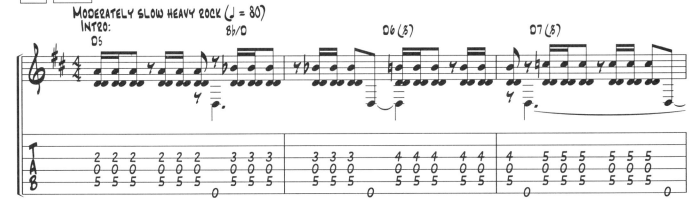

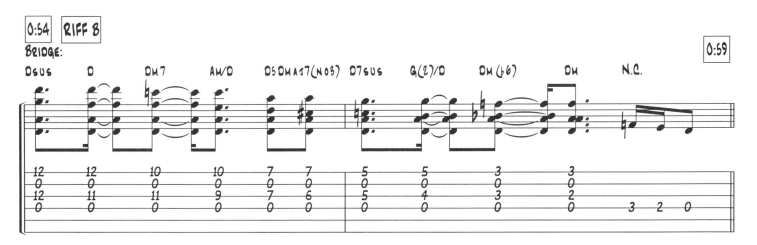

Living Loving Maid
(She's Just A Woman)
(Guitar Riff)

Music and Lyrics by
Jimmy Page and Robert Plant

© 1969 Flames of Albion Music, Inc.
Copyright Renewed
All Rights for Flames of Albion Music, Inc. Administered by WB MUSIC CORP.
All Rights Reserved

Misty Mountain Hop
(Guitar Riff)

Music and Lyrics by
Jimmy Page, Robert Plant
and John Paul Jones

© 1972 Flames of Albion Music, Inc.
Copyright Renewed
All Rights for Flames of Albion Music, Inc. Administered by WB MUSIC CORP.
All Rights Reserved

MOBY DICK
(Guitar Riff)

Gtr. in Drop D tuning:
⑥ = D ③ = G
⑤ = A ② = B
④ = D ① = E

Music by
Jimmy Page, John Bonham
and John Paul Jones

THE OCEAN
(Guitar Riff)

MUSIC AND LYRICS BY
JIMMY PAGE, ROBERT PLANT,
JOHN PAUL JONES AND JOHN BONHAM

ROCK AND ROLL
(Guitar Riff)

MUSIC AND LYRICS BY
JIMMY PAGE, ROBERT PLANT,
JOHN PAUL JONES AND JOHN BONHAM

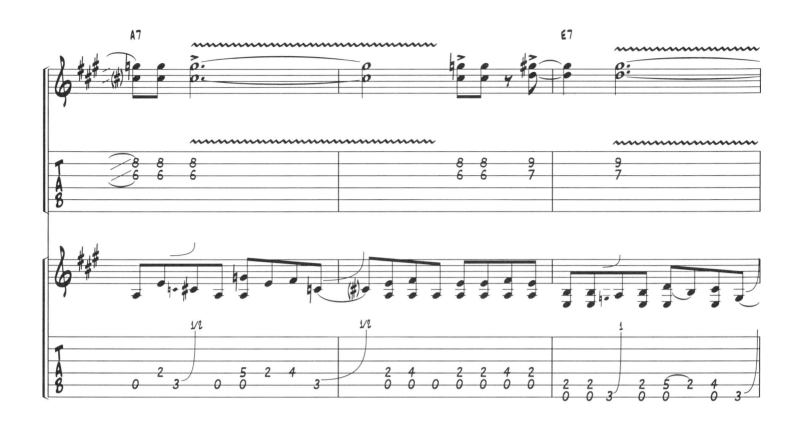

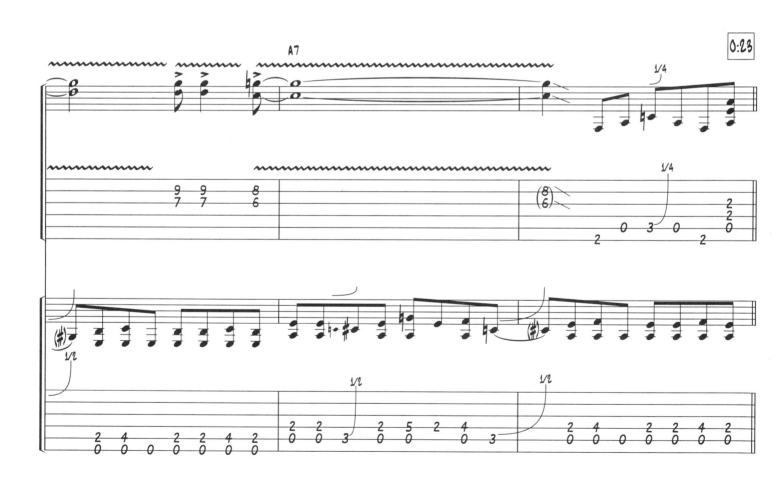

OVER THE HILLS AND FAR AWAY
(Guitar Riff)

Music and Lyrics by
Jimmy Page and Robert Plant

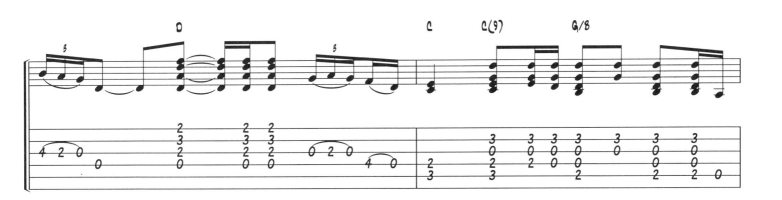

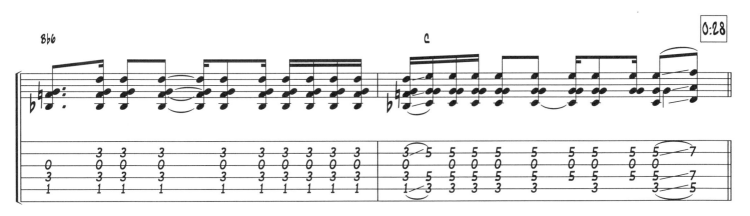

FBM0007

STAIRWAY TO HEAVEN
(Guitar Intro)

MUSIC AND LYRICS BY
JIMMY PAGE AND ROBERT PLANT

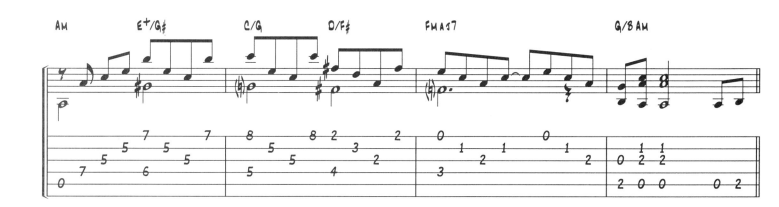

TANGERINE
(GUITAR RIFF)

MUSIC AND LYRICS BY
JIMMY PAGE

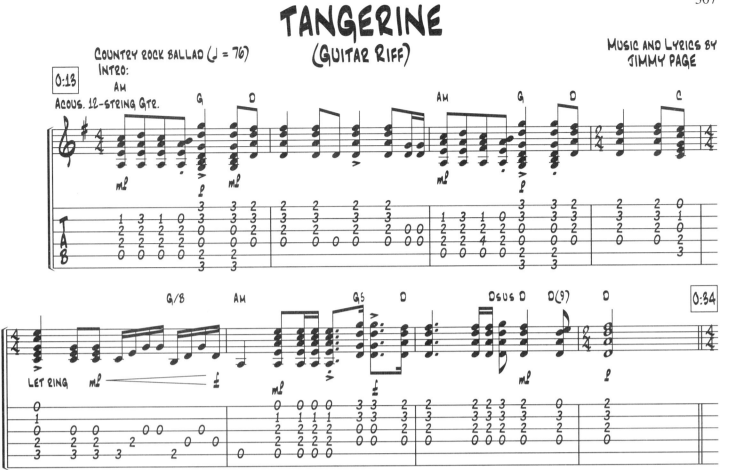

WHEN THE LEVEE BREAKS
(GUITAR RIFF)

MUSIC AND LYRICS BY
JIMMY PAGE, ROBERT PLANT,
JOHN PAUL JONES, JOHN BONHAM
AND MEMPHIS MINNIE

Elec. 12-string gtr. tuned to
Open G down a whole step:
⑥ = C   ③ = F
⑤ = F   ② = A
④ = C   ① = C

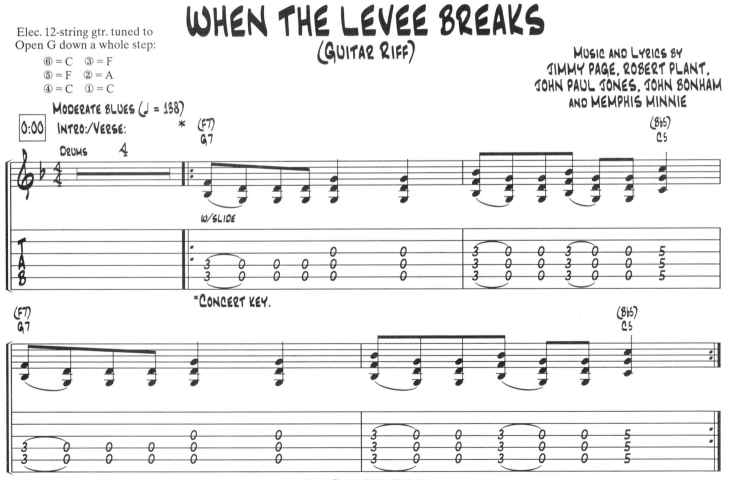

FBM0007

THE LEMON SONG
(Guitar Riff)

Music and Lyrics by
Jimmy Page, Robert Plant,
John Paul Jones and John Bonham

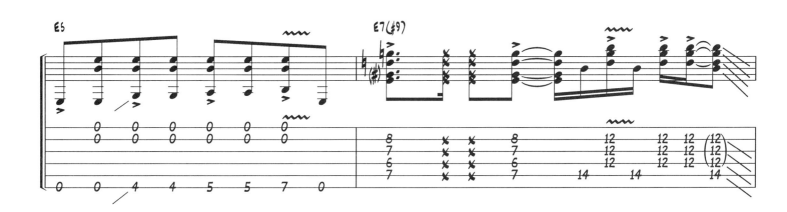
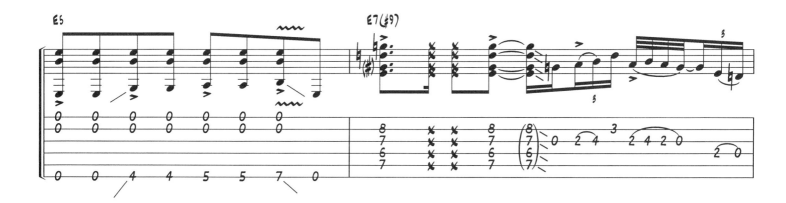
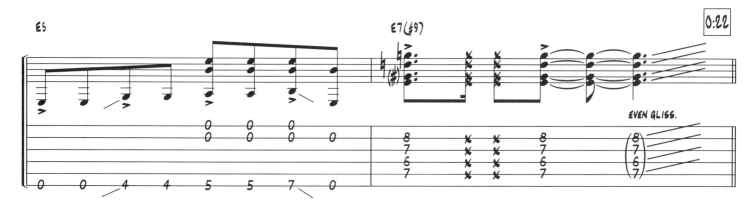

FBM0007

THE WANTON SONG
(Guitar Riff)

Music and Lyrics by
Jimmy Page and Robert Plant

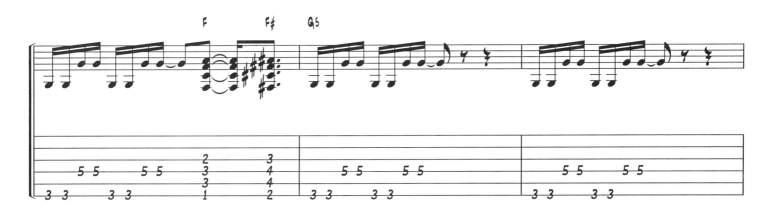

FBM0007

WHOLE LOTTA LOVE
(Guitar Riff)

Music and Lyrics by
Jimmy Page, Robert Plant,
John Paul Jones and John Bonham

YOUR TIME IS GONNA COME
(Guitar Riff)

Music and Lyrics by
Jimmy Page and John Paul Jones

FBM0007

OUT ON THE TILES
(Guitar Riff)

Music and Lyrics by
Jimmy Page, Robert Plant
and John Bonham

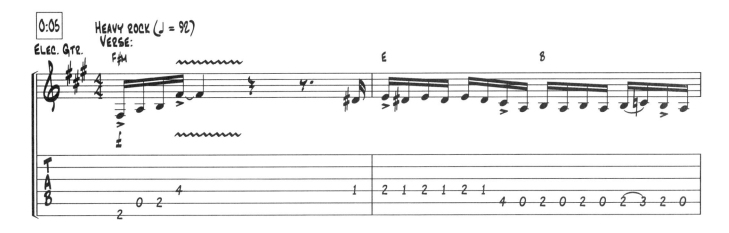

FBM0007

SELECTED SOLOS
Selected Solos

BABE, I'M GONNA LEAVE YOU
(GUITAR SOLO)

Music and Lyrics by
ANNE BREDON, JIMMY PAGE,
AND ROBERT PLANT

DAZED AND CONFUSED
(Guitar Solo)

Music and Lyrics by
Jimmy Page

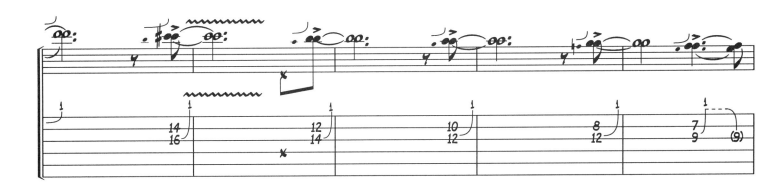

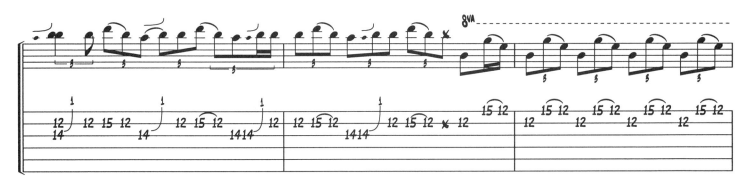

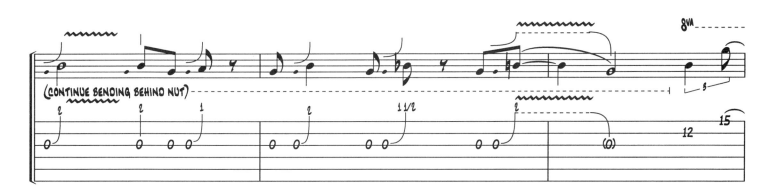

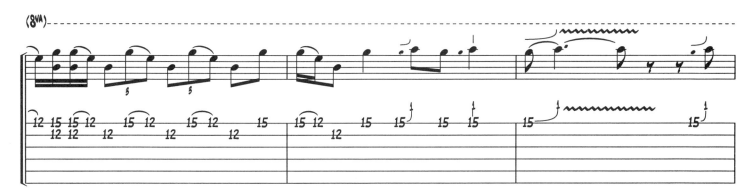

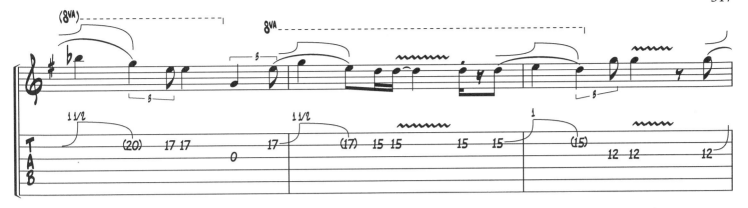

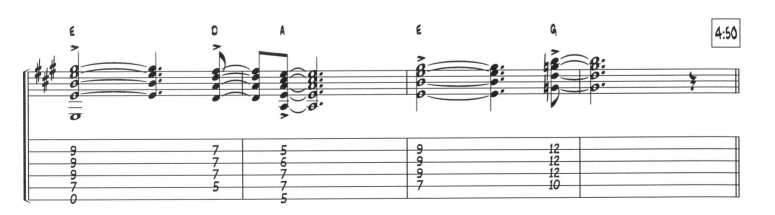

GOOD TIMES BAD TIMES
(Guitar Solo)

Music and Lyrics by
Jimmy Page, John Paul Jones
and John Bonham

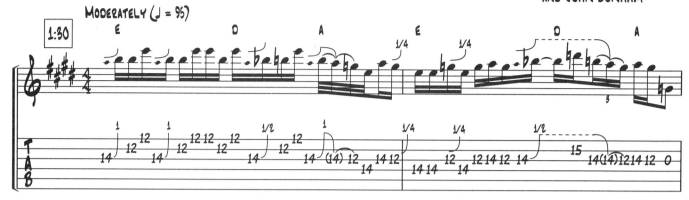

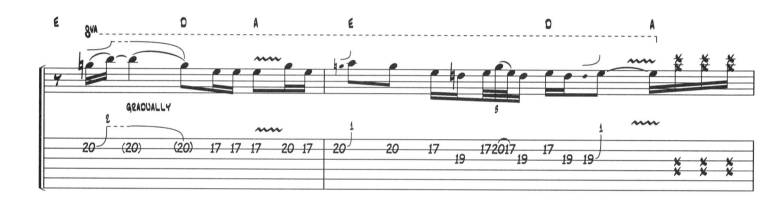

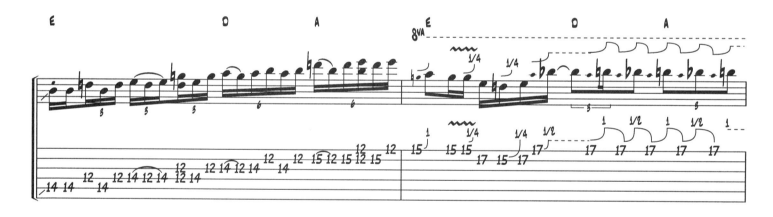

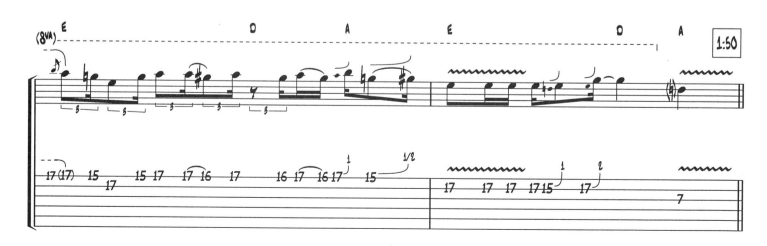

How Many More Times
(Guitar Solo)

Music and Lyrics by
Jimmy Page, John Paul Jones
and John Bonham

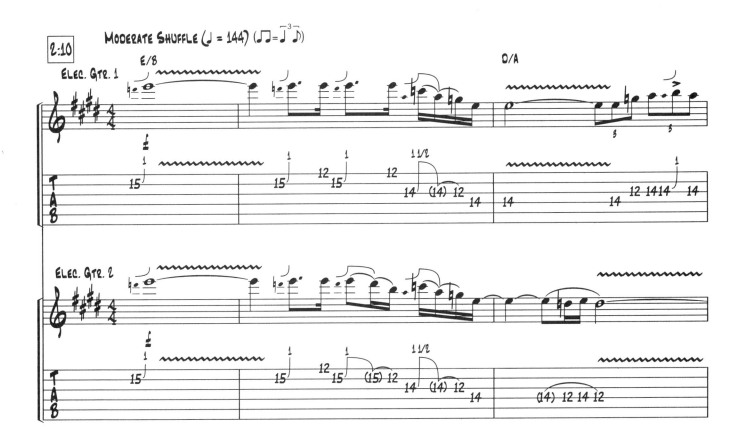

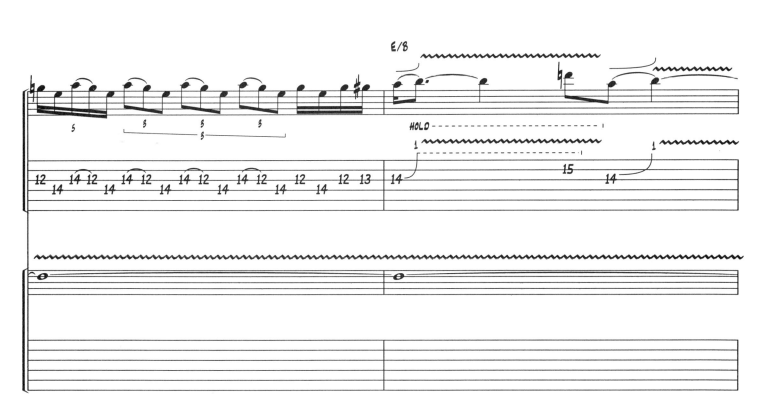

FBM0007

*BEND FROM BEHIND THE NUT.

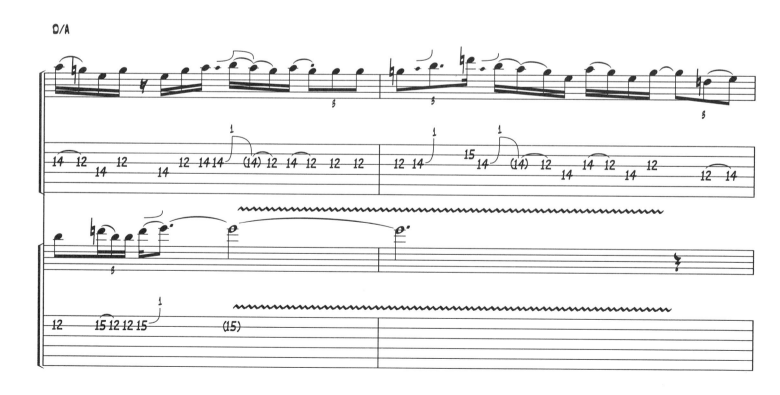

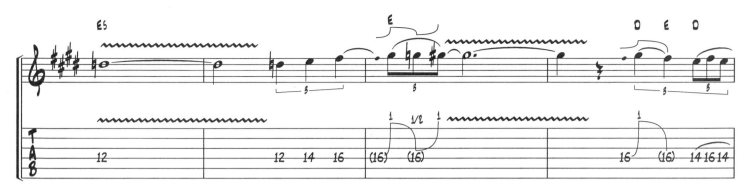

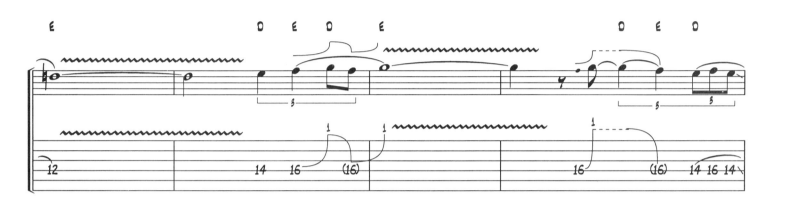

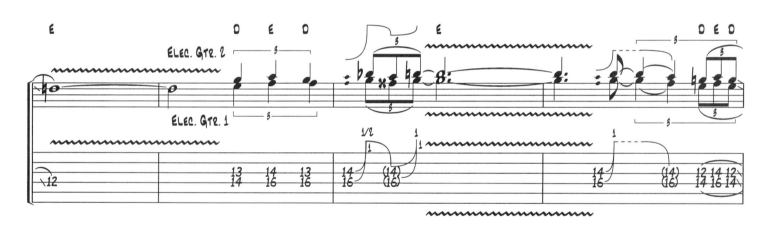

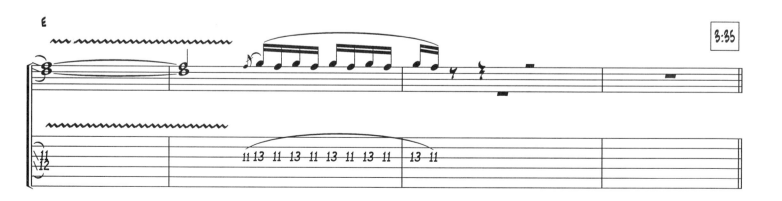

FBM0007

HEARTBREAKER
(Guitar Solo 1)

Music and Lyrics by
Jimmy Page, Robert Plant,
John Paul Jones and John Bonham

*Bend strings behind nut w/R.H.

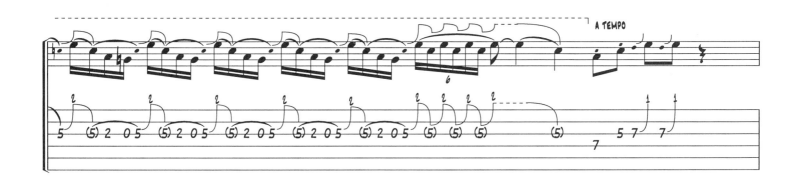

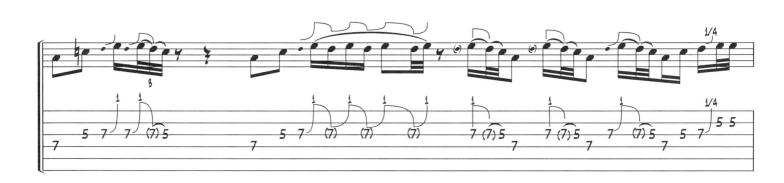

FBM0007

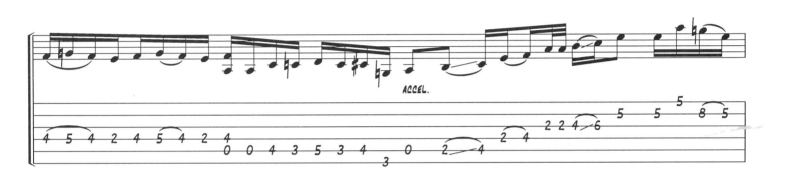

FBM0007

HEARTBREAKER
(Guitar Solo 2)

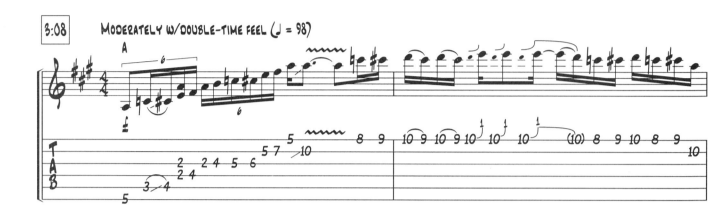

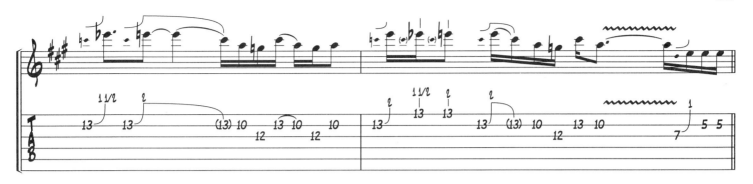

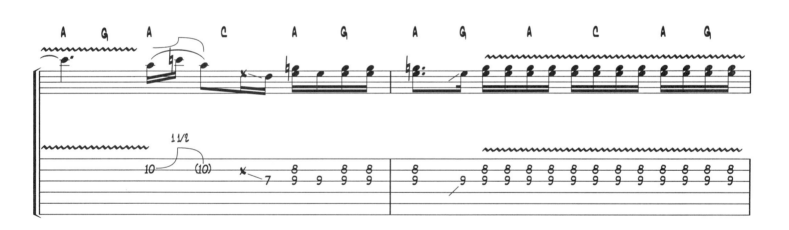

I CAN'T QUIT YOU BABY
(Guitar Solo)

Words and Music by
WILLIE DIXON

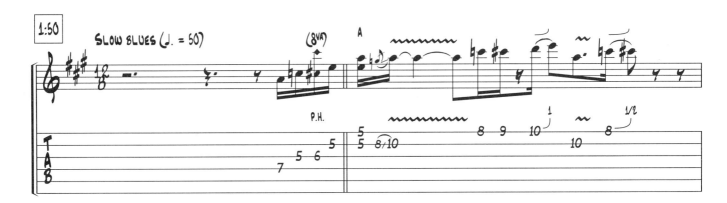

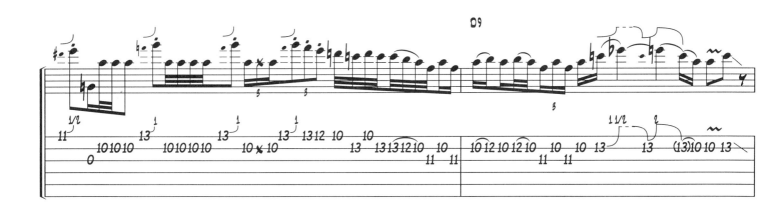

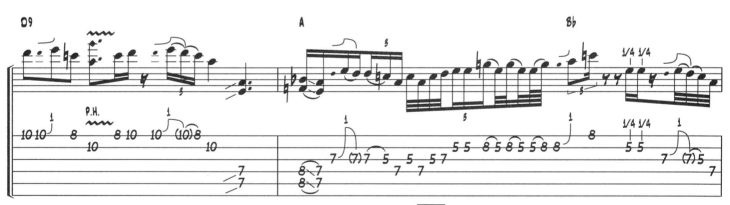

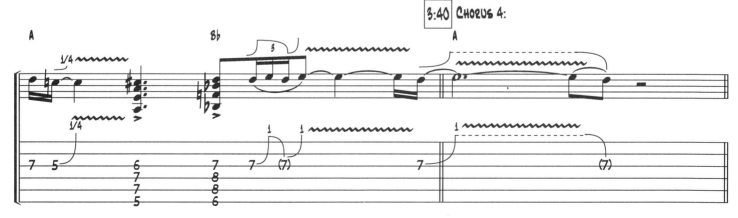

FBM0007

WHOLE LOTTA LOVE
(GUITAR SOLO)

Music and Lyrics by
Jimmy Page, Robert Plant,
John Paul Jones and John Bonham

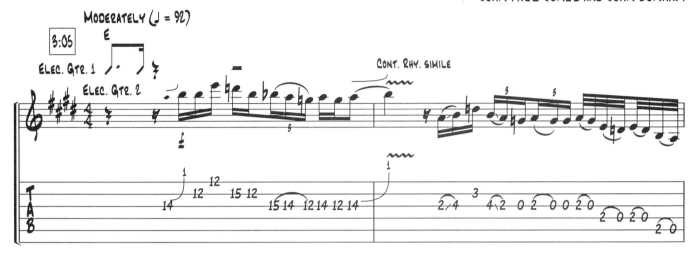

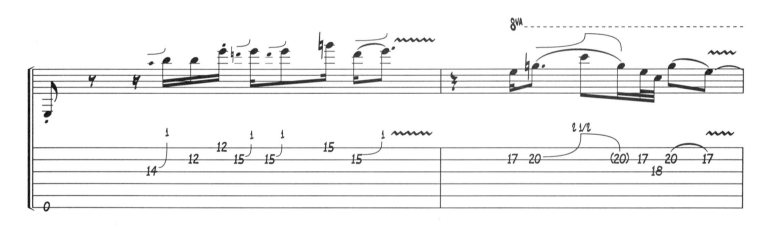

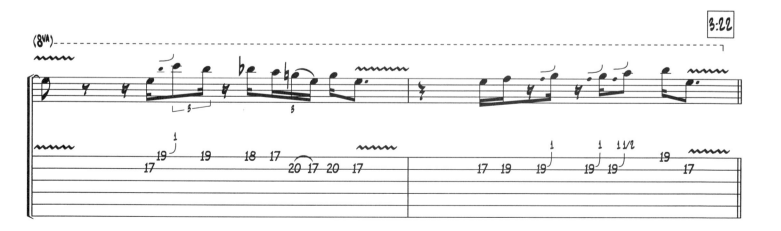

OVER THE HILLS AND FAR AWAY
(Guitar Solo)

MUSIC AND LYRICS BY
JIMMY PAGE AND ROBERT PLANT

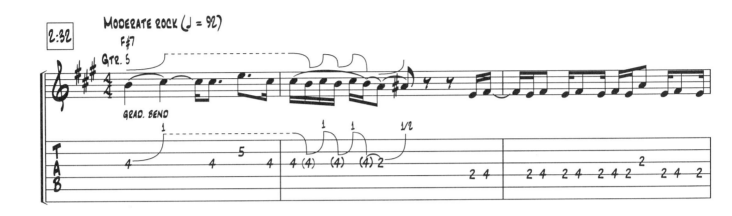

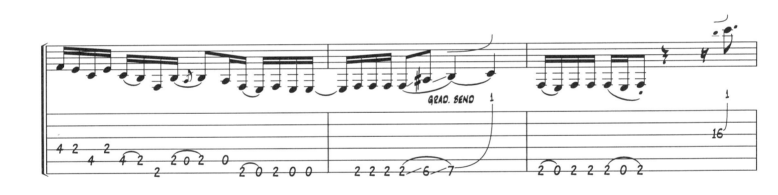

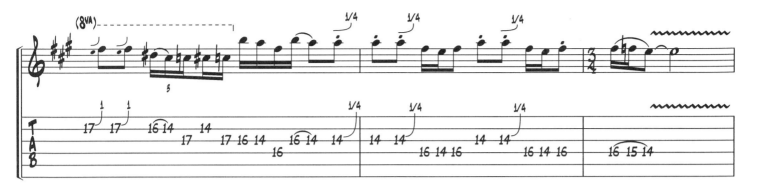

*Arranged for one guitar.

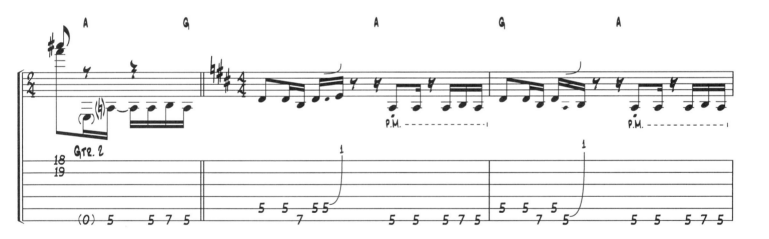

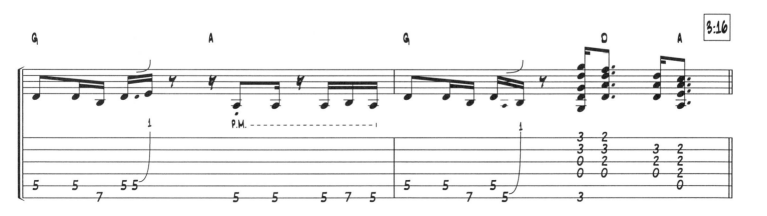

ROCK AND ROLL
(Guitar Solo)

MUSIC AND LYRICS BY
JIMMY PAGE, ROBERT PLANT,
JOHN PAUL JONES AND JOHN BONHAM

*TWO GTRS. ARR. FOR ONE.

FBM0007

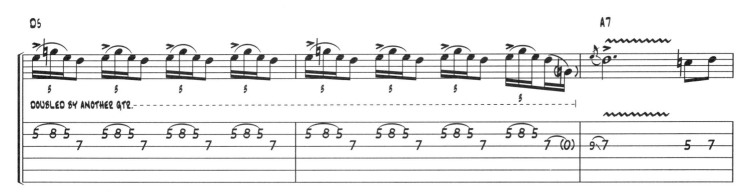

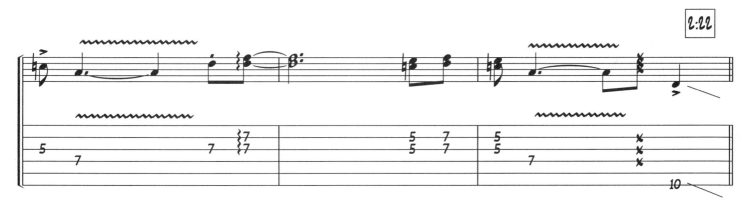

Since I've Been Loving You
(Guitar Solo)

Music and Lyrics by
Jimmy Page, Robert Plant
and John Paul Jones

STAIRWAY TO HEAVEN
(Guitar Solo)

MUSIC AND LYRICS BY
JIMMY PAGE AND ROBERT PLANT

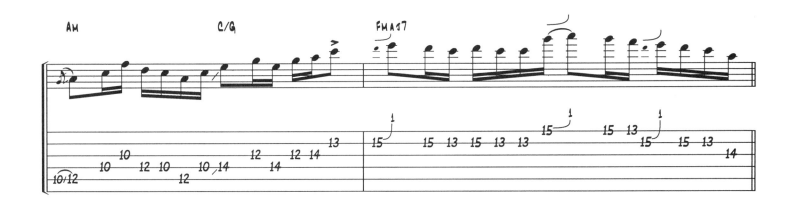

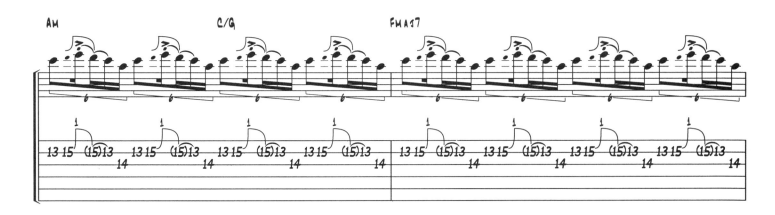

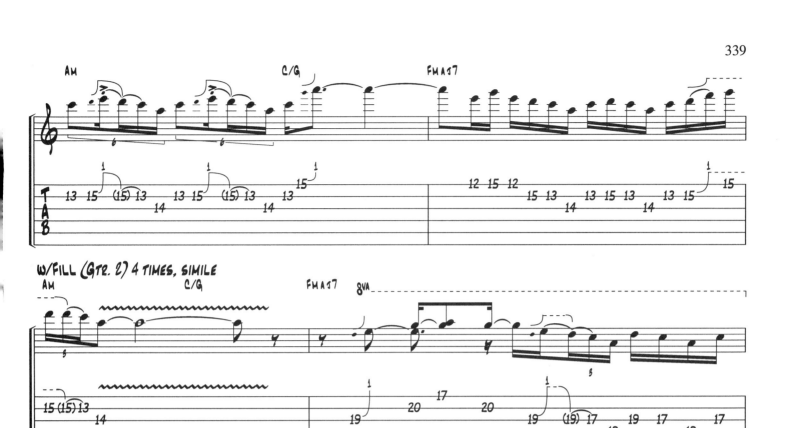

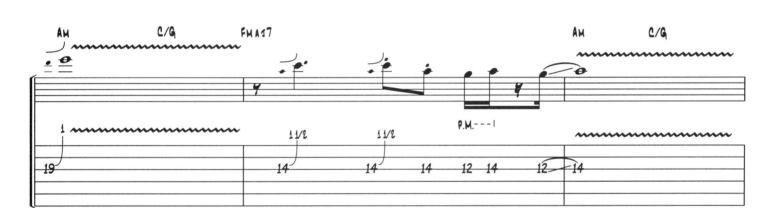

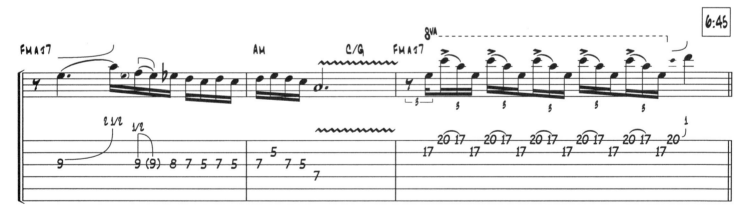

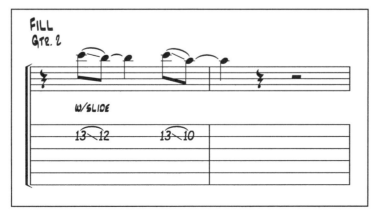

WHAT IS AND WHAT SHOULD NEVER BE
(Guitar Solo)

Music and Lyrics by
Jimmy Page and Robert Plant

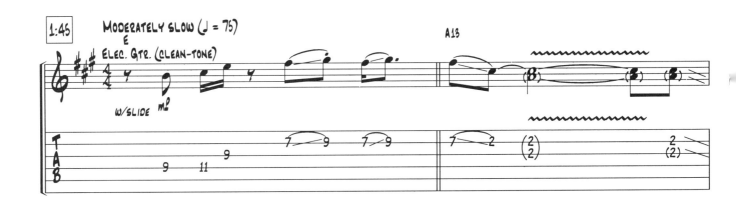

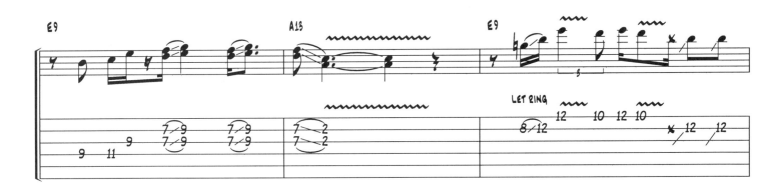

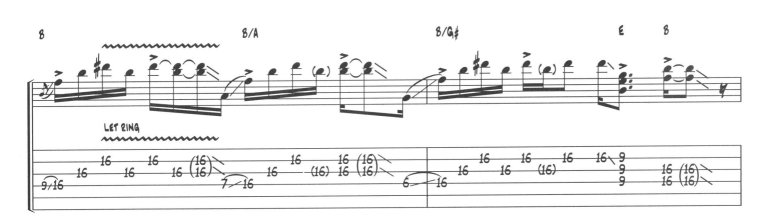

ALBUM INDEX

*Due to copyright restrictions, we are unable to include "We're Gonna Groove" in this collection.

The *Just Classic Rock Real Book* features 250 rock songs.

AFTER MIDNIGHT
AFTER THE GOLD RUSH
AGAINST THE WIND
AJA
ALL I WANT TO DO IS MAKE LOVE
   TO YOU
ALL RIGHT NOW
ALL THE YOUNG DUDES
AND IT STONED ME
ANGEL OF HARLEM
AQUALUNG
BABE, I'M GONNA LEAVE YOU
BAD MEDICINE
BAD MOON RISING
BAD TO THE BONE
THE BEAT GOES ON
BELL BOTTOM BLUES
BENNIE AND THE JETS
BETH
BIG LOVE
BIG YELLOW TAXI
BLAZE OF GLORY
BLEED TO LOVE HER
BORDER SONG
BORN ON THE BAYOU
BORN TO BE WILD
BOTH SIDES NOW
BOX OF RAIN
THE BOYS ARE BACK IN TOWN
ANOTHER BRICK IN THE WALL
   (Part 2)
BRIDGE OF SIGHS
BROKEN ARROW
BROWN EYED GIRL
CALIFORNIA
CALIFORNIA DREAMIN'
CALL ME
CANDLE IN THE WIND
CAN'T FIND MY WAY HOME
CARAVAN
CASEY JONES
CAT'S IN THE CRADLE
THE CHAIN
CHANGES
CHEAP SUNGLASSES
CHINA GROVE
CINNAMON GIRL
COCAINE
COME MONDAY
COMFORTABLY NUMB
COPPERLINE
COUNTRY GIRL
CRAZY LOVE
CREEQUE ALLEY
CROSS-EYED MARY
DANCING IN THE DARK
DANCING WITH MYSELF
DANIEL
DANNY'S SONG
DEACON BLUES

DEAR MR. FANTASY
DETROIT ROCK CITY
DEUCE
DO IT AGAIN
DO YOU WANT TO KNOW A
   SECRET
DON'T COME AROUND HERE
   NO MORE
DON'T LET THE SUN GO DOWN
   ON ME
DON'T STOP BELIEVIN'
DOWN ON THE CORNER
DRIVE
EUROPA (Earth's Cry Heaven's Smile)
EVERYBODY HURTS
EVIL WAYS
EYES WITHOUT A FACE
A FACE IN THE CROWD
FAITHFULLY
FAME
FIRE
FIRE LAKE
THE FIRST CUT IS THE DEEPEST
FOR WHAT IT'S WORTH
FORTUNATE SON
FOUNTAIN OF SORROW
FREE BIRD
FRIEND OF THE DEVIL
FUNK 49
GIMME ALL YOUR LOVIN'
GIMME SOME LOVIN'
GIMME THREE STEPS
GO YOUR OWN WAY
GOLDEN YEARS
GOOD TIMES ROLL
GOODBYE YELLOW BRICK ROAD
GOT ME UNDER PRESSURE
GREEN RIVER
HARVEST MOON
HAVE A CIGAR
HAVE YOU EVER SEEN THE RAIN?
HEART OF GOLD
HELP ME
HERE COME THOSE TEARS AGAIN
A HORSE WITH NO NAME
HOT FOR TEACHER
HOTEL CALIFORNIA
HOUSE AT POOH CORNER
HOUSE OF THE RISING SUN
HUNGRY HEART
I CAN'T TELL YOU WHY
I GOT YOU BABE
I KNOW YOU RIDER
I STILL HAVEN'T FOUND WHAT
   I'M LOOKING FOR
I WANNA BE SEDATED
I WANT TO HOLD YOUR HAND
I WON'T BACK DOWN
I'M JUST A SINGER (In a Rock and
   Roll Band)
I'D LOVE TO CHANGE THE WORLD
I'M A MAN
I'M ON FIRE
IN-A-GADDA-DA-VIDA
INTO THE MYSTIC
JAMIE'S CRYIN'
JOHN BARLEYCORN
JOSIE
JUMP

JUST WHAT I NEEDED
KEY TO THE HIGHWAY
LA GRANGE
LAYLA
LEGS
LEVON
LIFE IN THE FAST LANE
LIKE A ROCK
LISTEN TO THE MUSIC
LOCOMOTIVE BREATH
LONG DISTANCE RUN AROUND
LONG TRAIN RUNNIN'
LOSING MY RELIGION
A LOVE SONG
THE LOW SPARK OF HIGH
   HEELED BOYS
LVIN' ON A PRAYER
LYIN' EYES
MAGIC CARPET RIDE
MAN ON THE MOON
MARGARITAVILLE
MEXICO
MILLWORKER
MINUTE BY MINUTE
MONEY
MOONDANCE
MORE THAN A FEELING
MY BEST FRIEND'S GIRL
MY HOMETOWN
MY OLD SCHOOL
NEVER GOING BACK AGAIN
NEW YEAR'S DAY
NIGHT MOVES
THE NIGHT THEY DROVE OLD
   DIXIE DOWN
NIGHTS IN WHITE SATIN
OH, PRETTY WOMAN
OHIO
OLD MAN
OLD TIME ROCK & ROLL
ONE OF THESE NIGHTS
ONE WAY OR ANOTHER
OPEN ARMS
OWNER OF A LONELY HEART
PANAMA
PEACEFUL EASY FEELING
PEG
PEOPLE GET READY
PINK CADILLAC
PLEASE, PLEASE ME
PRESENCE OF THE LORD
THE PRETENDER
PRIDE (In the Name of Love)
PROUD MARY
QUESTION
REBEL YELL
REELIN' IN THE YEARS
RIDE MY SEE-SAW
RIKKI DON'T LOSE THAT
   NUMBER
THE ROAD
ROCK & ROLL BAND
ROCK FAND ROLL ALL NITE
ROCK AND ROLL NEVER
   FORGETS
ROCK ME ON THE WATER
ROCK 'N' ROLL HIGH SCHOOL
ROCKET MAN
ROCKY MOUNTAIN WAY

ROUNDABOUT
RUNNIN' DOWN A DREAM
RUNNIN' WITH THE DEVIL
RUNNING ON EMPTY
SAN FRANCISCO
SATURDAY NIGHT SPECIAL
SEA OF JOY
SHARP DRESSED MAN
SHE'S NOT THERE
SHEENA IS A PUNK ROCKER
SHINY HAPPY PEOPLE
SISTER GOLDEN HAIR
SOCIETY'S CHILD
SOMEONE SAVED MY LIFE
   TONIGHT
SOUTHERN MAN
SPOONFUL
STAGE FRIGHT
STOP DRAGGIN' MY HEART
   AROUND
THE STORY IN YOUR EYES
STRANGE BREW
STREETS OF PHILADELPHIA
STRUTTER
SUFFRAGETTE CITY
SUNDAY BLOODY SUNDAY
SUNSHINE OF YOUR LOVE
SWEET HOME ALABAMA
TAKE IT EASY
TAKE IT TO THE LIMIT
TAKIN' IT TO THE STREETS
TALES OF BRAVE ULYSSES
TAXI
TEACHER
TEARS IN HEAVEN
TELL HER NO
TENTH AVENUE FREEZE-OUT
TEQUILA SUNRISE
THESE DREAMS
TIME OF THE SEASON
TIN MAN
TINY DANCER
TONIGHT SHE COMES
TUESDAY AFTERNOON
TURN TURN TURN
UNCLE JOHN'S BAND
UNFAITHFUL SERVANT
UP ON CRIPPLE CREEK
VENTURA HIGHWAY
THE WAITING
WANTED DEAD OR ALIVE
WHAT A FOOL BELIEVES
WHAT'S YOUR NAME
WHEN LOVE COMES TO TOWN
WHERE THE STREETS HAVE
   NO NAME
WHITE ROOM
WHITE WEDDING
A WHITER SHADE OF PALE
WHO'S CRYING NOW
WHY DON'T WE GET DRUNK
WILD NIGHT
WISH YOU WERE HERE
WITH OR WITHOUT YOU
WOODSTOCK
YOU GIVE LOVE A BAD NAME
YOU GOT LUCKY
YOU REALLY GOT ME
YOUR SONG